Women in Educat

Edited by Janet Ouston

LONGMAN

Longman Information and Reference
Longman Group UK Limited,
The High, Harlow, Essex, CM20 1YR, England
and Associated Companies Throughout the World.
Telephone Harlow (0279) 442601; Fax Harlow (0279) 444501;
Telex 81491 Padlog

First published 1993

A catalogue record for this book is available from the British Library

ISBN 0–582–10190–5

Printed and bound in Great Britain by
Biddles Ltd, Guildford and King's Lynn

Contents

Preface

Twelve years ago I met a formidable inspector of education in Sweden. Through encouragement, training and hard work this person had championed the promotion of women to headships in Stockholm and had succeeded dramatically in encouraging more women to apply for promotion and more selectors to change their prejudices and preconceptions.

I hope that this book may have a similar impact. It is important to encourage women to apply for promotion. It is also vital to influence the thinking and practice of professional and lay selectors. The improvement of educational institutions and the creation of dynamic and creative places of learning requires a drive to recruit and develop leadership of the highest quality. No longer can we afford to squander half of our potential leadership in schools and colleges. The effort to make the changes required will involve review of policies and practice. Above all it will require an understanding and a will to make those changes. This book makes a significant contribution to the development of thinking, policy and practice.

Derek Esp
Chair, BEMAS Publication Committee

List of Contributors

Hilary Atchison is National Education Adviser, Oxfam, Oxford; formerly Advisory Teacher, London Borough of Hounslow.

Anne Gold is Lecturer, Management Development Centre, Institute of Education, University of London.

Peggy Gosling is Lecturer, Syracuse University (London Centre) and Visiting Tutor, Management Development Centre, Institute of Education, University of London.

Valerie Hall is Lecturer, National Development Centre for Educational Management and Policy, University of Bristol.

Helen McMullan is Head of Year, Hayes Manor School, Hayes, Middlesex

Janet Ouston is Head of Centre and Senior Lecturer, Management Development Centre, Institute of Education, University of London.

Anne Segall is Career Development Manager, British Broadcasting Corporation.

Charol Shakeshaft is Professor and Chairperson, Administration and Policy Studies, Hofstra University, New York.

1 Women as managers

Janet Ouston

This book explores many different aspects of the current position of women in the management of education. Its chapters are diverse and its contributors come from several different backgrounds. What they have in common is their concern about women's under-representation in management roles, and an optimism that this need not necessarily continue.

After this introductory chapter, Anne Gold (Chapter 2) reflects on 'the slippery discourses' used in thinking and talking about women in education management. Research in the UK is reviewed by Valerie Hall (Chapter 3), and Charol Shakeshaft describes her recent work in the USA (Chapter 4). Helen McMullan then reports a study of the position of women teachers in five secondary schools (Chapter 5).

The second half of the book starts with an analysis by Anne Gold of the Management Development Centre's management programmes (Chapter 6), and Hilary Atchison reflects on her work in a Local Education Authority (Chapter 7). There is very little research on the development of managers in education: a study in this area is reported by Janet Ouston, Anne Gold and Peggy Gosling (Chapter 8). Anne Segall's chapter (Chapter 9) on her work at the BBC is the only one that comes from outside education. It shows how the issues we are so familiar with in education are not unique. The BBC's progress over a ten year period in increasing the number of women in top management grades should encourage us to continue to research, discuss, debate and argue for more equitable patterns of promotion in education. With the exception of Charol Shakeshaft's chapter on research in the USA, all the contributions reflect English experience.

Underpinning the whole book is the fact that women are under-represented in management roles. This chapter starts by presenting extracts from educational statistics since 1988 to examine the proportion of women and men who are headteachers and hold incentive allowances. It then explores some common themes that emerge from recent studies of women in management, drawing on research in education and elsewhere to illustrate the issues. Detailed exploration of these themes is left to subsequent chapters.

The current position

Statistical data on the employment of women in schools demonstrates how women are under-represented in senior posts. The percentages of women teachers are shown in Table 1.1.

Table 1.1 – Proportion of women teachers

	1988 %	**1989** %	**1990** %	**1991** %
In primary schools	79.8	80.2	80.7	81.0
In secondary schools	45.6	45.9	46.4	46.9

Data from *DES Statistics of Education: Schools 1988, 1989, 1990, and 1991.*

Four out of five primary school teachers are women, and just under half of secondary school teachers. Over the four year period from 1988 to 1991 the proportion of women teachers has risen very slightly in both sectors.

If men and women were fully represented in headships it might be expected that four fifths of primary schools, and half secondary schools would have women heads. But this is not the case, as shown in Table 1.2.

Table 1.2 – Schools and headship

	1988 %	**1989** %	**1990** %	**1991** %
Primary schools with women heads	46.7	47.2	47.9	48.5
Secondary schools with women heads	16.5	16.9	17.1	18.3

Data from *DES Statistics of Education: Schools 1988, 1989, 1990 and 1991.*

Just under half of the primary schools in England and Wales have a woman headteacher. In secondary schools around one in six schools has a woman head. But the percentages of women have increased slightly in both sectors since 1988.

Al-Khalifa (1989) points out that the proportion of women heads declined through the 1960s and 1970s. With the move to co-educational comprehensive schools women who were heads of single sex schools were replaced by men in mixed schools. In recent years the proportion of women heads in mixed secondary schools has risen, as shown in Table 1.3.

Table 1.3 – Mixed secondary schools only

	1988 %	1989 %	1990 %	1991 %
Mixed secondary schools with women heads	9.5	12.5	13.4	14.2

Data from *DES Statistics of Education: Schools 1988, 1989, 1990 and 1991.*

It is also possible to consider the relative position of men and women in terms of their distribution across the staffing structure as a whole. Table 1.4 shows that in primary schools just under one-third of male teachers are heads, compared to one in 14 women teachers.

The differential is also marked in secondary schools: one in 30 male teachers is a head compared to less than one in a 100 women teachers. These figures have remained very similar across the four year period.

Table 1.4 – Proportion of teachers who are heads

	1988 %	1989 %	1990 %	1991 %
Male primary heads/male primary teachers	31.7	31.6	31.5	31.5
Female primary heads/ female primary teachers	7.0	7.0	6.9	7.0
Male secondary heads/male secondary teachers	3.3	3.5	3.4	3.5
Female secondary heads/ female secondary teachers	0.8	0.8	0.8	0.9

Data from *DES Statistics of Education: Schools 1988, 1989, 1990 and 1991.*

The under-representation of women in both sectors is also apparent in the distribution of incentive allowances as shown in Table 1.5.

Again the data show considerable differentials with women under-represented in senior posts and over-represented among those with no allowances.

To sum up, there are marked differences between men and women in the proportions holding senior posts. There is some evidence that women are improving their position, but much remains to be achieved. It should also be noted that only full-time teachers are included in the tables; approximately 15 per cent of teachers are part-timers, and 85 per cent of these are women.

Table 1.5 – Proportion of men and women teachers with incentive allowances

	Men			Women		
	1989 %	1990 %	1991 %	1989 %	1990 %	1991 %
Primary schools						
Deputy head, D and E	18.2	19.5	19	8.6	8.7	9
A, B and C	19.4	23.9	25	21.8	30.3	33
No incentive allowance	28.2	24.0	23	62.1	53.3	51
Secondary schools						
Deputy head, D and E	31.3	31.9	32	13.3	13.9	14
A, B and C	35.9	39.3	41	36.4	43.5	47
No incentive allowance	28.9	24.7	23	49.2	41.4	38

1989 and 1990 data from *DES Statistics of Education: Teachers in Service in England and Wales, 1989 and 1990*. 1991 data from *School Teachers' Review Body: Second Report, February 1993*: only available rounded to the nearest whole number. Data are not yet published for 1992.

Governing bodies, too, tend to be male dominated. A recent study of 16 governing bodies (Buckby 1992) showed that around three quarters of the governors were men. Men tended to be older than women governors and to have served on the governing body for a longer period: half of the men had served for more than six years, compared to one-quarter of the women.

Why?

Why should women collectively find themselves so poorly represented in management roles? Schmuck (1986) identified three sets of concepts that have been used to understand women's under-representation in senior posts in education: the socialisation of women, organisational constraints on women's promotion and theories relating to gender-based careers. We might also add to this the socialisation of men, and men's powerful definitions of the world of work.

Spencer and Podmore (1987) in their interesting collection of essays on women in male-dominated professions identified 'ten factors which contribute to the professional marginalisation of women . . . some of which are closely interlinked' (p. 2).

The ten points are summarised below:

- stereotypes about women, that they are unstable, emotional, not decisive enough;
- stereotypes about the nature of professions and professionals, that women are unsuited to the demands of the job;

- the sponsorship system, the lack of older women to support younger women;
- the lack of role models and peers;
- women being excluded from informal relationships and networks;
- the concept of professional commitment, and the assumption that women will not be committed enough;
- the unplanned nature of many women's careers;
- the assumptions made about what is 'women's work';
- clients' expectations — that women are unacceptable in certain roles;
- fear of competition, that women will reduce the prestige of the profession.

Teachers are not in a male-dominated profession, but much of the research about women in management generally, and women in education management, raises similar issues. Two quotations from research projects on women in management outside education sum up men's advantage in obtaining senior posts:

> 'Men are assumed to possess any necessary competence, until such time as they demonstrate otherwise, but women need most positively to establish the fact of their competence before this will be recognised.' (Spencer 1987, p. 134)

Coe's survey (1992) of managers in commercial organisations showed that attitudes to women were a major issue in their promotion. On its publication the Director of the Institute of Management commented:

> 'Men are still the prime barrier to women in management. Despite some progress, old fashioned sexist attitudes are still common and represent a real, not imagined, barrier to the progress of women'. (Press release, Coe 1992)

Is this true in education, too? What other factors lead to the position of women in education which is so apparent from the statistics?

Recent findings in commercial management

Nationally only 3 per cent of senior managers and around 9 per cent of general managers were women; just under half of those in paid employment were women (British Institute of Management, 1992). It is not possible to make direct comparisons between these statistics and posts of responsibility in schools, but they are similar to the proportion of women holding incentive allowances D and above in secondary schools.

In 1992 the Institute of Management carried out a survey of all women members of the Institute and a random sample of men. Their report (Coe 1992) is based on the replies of 1,500 women and 800 men. The findings will be included at several points in this chapter where they appear to be relevant to women in education management. A similar, large scale study of members of the Institute was also undertaken by Alban-Metcalfe and West (1991). Both surveys explored the factors which enabled and impeded women in their progress to senior management posts.

Do women have a different management style to men?

This issue is reviewed in detail by Valerie Hall and Charol Shakeshaft later in this book. In general researchers report that there are differences between men and women in their management style, but there is considerable overlap, too. The practical issue seems to be whether working groups of men and women can build on the similarities, or whether the differences impair the group's performance and undermine women's self esteem.

Eagley, Karau and Johnson (1992) report a meta-analysis of 50 studies of gender and leadership style. The main finding was that women have a more participatory, democratic, style. They also reported that women are more task focused, more concerned with students and learning than men.

Vinnicombe (1987) reported that the major difference found in her psychometrics-based survey of men and women managers was the lack of 'traditionalists' among the women. Only 26 per cent of them were placed in this category compared to over half the men. Women managers were more likely to be 'visionaries' and 'catalysts'.

Recent work in managerial competences (Esp 1993) makes no distinction between men and women. The long lists of competences developed by different groups include both stereotypically male and female tasks. The key issue here is not the content of the lists, but the ways in which competences are assessed. Will men and women differ in their perceptions of their own performance, and will they vary in their assessments of others?

Research suggests that there are real differences between men and women in their management styles and that women have an important and different contribution to make to the management of schools. But women are often not given the permission (or the power) to extend men's experience of the management of schools. Women have to maintain and celebrate their strengths, while enabling men and women to understand and experience what they can offer.

Women's attitudes to their careers

In the past it has been said that women are not committed to their careers, but recent surveys give no support to this view. Coe (1992) reported very few differences between men and women in their perceptions of their career progression.

Aisenberg and Harrington's (1988) thought-provoking book is based on in depth interviews with 25 women academics mostly post-graduate students or junior academic staff. They identify a different kind of commitment from that typically reported by men: for the women their academic work was part of their own transformation and liberation and this led to their focus on the humanities. 'Women jumping into the male-defined practical fields may not gain power but may risk losing the self' (p. 90).

Alban-Metcalfe and West (1991) compared the satisfaction that men and women report from their jobs: women rate aspects of satisfaction from the job itself more highly than men; men rate fringe benefits, earnings and security more highly than women.

Micro-politics

Women may not be learning 'the rules of the game' for getting on in their organisation. Aisenberg and Harrington (1988) suggest that they hold to the 'merit dream', that promotion is achieved on the basis of merit and hard work. 'A lack of knowledge was coupled with a refusal to know, a shunning of political issues' (p. 52). These women reported a distaste for the politics and self-promotion required to succeed in university life.

Powney and Weiner (1991) identify the woman career 'drifter' who works hard and loyally for her organisation, expecting promotion as a reward. They do not, however, initiate career changes, but respond to those that become available.

Applicants for senior posts

It is often said that women lack confidence to apply for senior posts, but that those who do apply are more likely to be successful. Evidence from New Zealand supports this. The proportion of women teachers in New Zealand schools is very similar to those in England and Wales. Considering senior positions in secondary schools in 1990, 38 per cent of applications came from women and 52 per cent of the appointees were women. At principal level women made 19 per cent of the applications and were 20 per cent of those appointed (Cusack 1992).

Less detailed information is available relating to England. Migniuolo (1992) quotes information from two LEA surveys which show that, while equal proportions of men and women apply for one promotion over a two year period, many more men make more than four applications.

Career paths

Men and women have different career paths. In education women tend to get into cross curricular, pastoral and support activities (Torrington and Weightman 1989, Coe 1992, and McBurney and Hough 1989) rather than in straight line management jobs which lead to senior posts. 'Men tend to do the high profile, straightforward jobs that are part of the natural progression up the hierarchy' (Weightman 1989, p. 121). A similar point emerged from the Institute of Management Survey (Coe 1992) where women were more likely to be in support functions such as personnel, education and training, marketing or administration. Only 1 per cent were in manufacturing or production, which are the usual routes to promotion.

In his study of LMS in primary schools Stainton (1992) raises a concern about women's promotion. Will male heads take over the 'business' of the school, leaving their women deputies to deal with teaching, pastoral and staffing issues, and as a consequence be less well prepared for promotion to headship?

Many women spend some of their working life in part-time jobs or take career breaks. DES statistics show that part-time teaching posts are nearly all held by women which excludes them from most promotions (DES 1988, 1989, 1990, 1991).

Career planning

Aisenberg and Harrington (1988) report that women are less likely to have a career map than men: women have goals but make ad hoc arrangements to get to them. Interviewees reported an intense commitment to their work, but were internally driven rather than instrumentally and externally driven. This led them to lose self-esteem if their work was criticised. Similarly Davidson and Cooper (1992) reported that women get more satisfaction from the tasks of work, and men from earnings, job security, and office politics. Women are likely to move more often throughout their careers, while men only do this early on (Alban-Metcalfe and West 1991). This echoes a finding from the Institute of Management survey where only 20 per cent of women saw internal promotion as the next step compared to 36 per cent of men.

Women's confidence

> Confidence is the key factor for every women in management. (McLoughlin 1992, p. 56)

The Management Development Centre started running management courses ten years ago. Ever since one of the major comments made in course evaluations is the impact that the programmes have on participants' confidence. This is particularly true for women. Other researchers, too, comment on women's lack of confidence in their management role, which seems to be due to the lack of a common perception of how a women in a management role should behave. There are often implicit agreements about how she should not behave: she is expected to never lose her temper, to remain cool, calm and 'ladylike'. Aisenberg and Harrington (1988) say that women have difficulty in developing an authoritative voice, they tend to be modest about achievements and knowledge and to only speak assertively when concerned about others. Able women consider themselves to be average and are not good at promoting themselves or their achievements. Powney and Weiner (1991) also identify confidence as 'the key to becoming and remaining a manager' (p. 12).

Travers and Cooper (1991) point out that the women in their study saw appraisal as a major source of stress. They suggest that this may result from women teachers' lack of confidence and lack of self-esteem. Research in other areas of employment has also pointed to women's disadvantage in appraisal. Alimo-Metcalf (1991) found that women managers in the National Health Service experienced greater difficulties in the appraisal process than did men.

McLoughlin (1992) stressed older women's lack of confidence, but reported that her younger women interviewees had an internal confidence which the older women had not achieved.

Work overload was the main source of stress reported by Davidson and Cooper (1992) in their survey of women managers. They interpreted this as partly due to women's need to prove themselves: to be seen to be competent. But Weightman's work discussed below suggests that some women are expected to take on more tasks than a man at the same level of seniority.

Job-related stress

Davidson and Cooper (1992) review the rapid changes that have occurred in recent years in the employment of women. Increasing numbers of women have been working in paid employment, but generally they are in low-status, low-paid jobs and often work part-time. It is still proving difficult for them to move into higher levels of management. Davidson and Cooper argue that there is a 'glass ceiling' for women to break through in management posts, and that this creates extra demands on them which are reflected in higher rates of stress-related illness.

In a large scale study of teachers, Travers and Cooper (1991) reported that women teachers suffered more job-related pressures than men, and had poorer mental health. Teachers as a whole had poorer mental health than other highly stressed professional groups such as dentists, GPs and tax inspectors. But women also reported higher levels of job satisfaction than men: the authors suggest that this may be because women get satisfaction from the task of teaching, accept poor promotion prospects and take career breaks, while men are more adversely influenced by negative external influences on schools such as the poor public image of teachers and the pace of imposed change.

Weightman (1989) said: 'We found in several schools a tendency for women to have two specific posts of responsibility at the same grade as men who had only one of the jobs' (p. 119). 'The women often had to do more for less by having a dual role or accepting a lower grading of similar work' (p. 121). This issue is discussed in Helen McMullan's chapter in this book.

Many studies of employed women comment on the stress on women of attempting to manage their multiple roles and the difficulty in achieving a 'balanced life' (Marshall 1984).

Women and children

> The real problems started after maternity leave. (Marshall 1984, p. 188)

Studies of women managers are increasingly drawing attention to the differences in their working lives between women without children and those with children. Although women generally have lower rates of coronary heart disease than men, married working women had higher rates than single women, with working women with children having the highest rates of all (Davidson and Cooper 1992).

Women managers reported that work overload was their major problem, with conflicts between home and work a second, major, issue. Most surveys find that women managers are only half as likely as male managers to be married and many more are divorced. Coe's survey (1992) of women members of the Institute of Management, for example, found that 68 per cent were married, compared to 92 per cent of men, and 12 per cent were divorced or separated (5 per cent men). Of the men and women who were married, 49 per cent of women had children compared to 86 per cent of men. More men (70 per cent) reported 'caring responsibilities' than women (37 per cent), but the women reported the much greater impact of caring on their careers. The main adverse effect for women was 'the difficulty in working long hours' and 'the need to work locally'. Similar figures were reported by Davidson and Cooper (1992).

Personal accounts by women of their careers (Whitehead 1993, for example) suggest that becoming a parent is a critical stage of a woman's professional development. For many women it creates role conflict, and the consequences of part-time employment are rarely positive. These problems may be resolved by mothers leaving their careers even if this was not their intention before they had children (Coward 1992). Other women resolve this issue by not having children, by working long hours that could not be combined with caring for a family (see Ozga 1993).

McLoughlin (1992), in her study of younger women in business, reports that most of her interviewees had postponed having children until they were well established in their careers. In general, they had only one child and earned enough to employ child carers.

Will the future demand a new management style and structure in schools?

As early as 1971 Schon argued that the stable state was breaking down and that the rate of change was accelerating. Survival and growth could only be ensured by becoming a 'learning' organisation. More recently research in general management (e.g. Peters and Waterman 1982, Pedler, Burgoyne and Boydell 1991) has argued that organisations need to become less bureaucratic and flatter in their structure, and more flexible in their operations, to be able to respond effectively to rapid internal and external change.

Caldwell and Spinks (1992), quoting Naisbitt and Aburdene (1990) and Sergiovanni (1990) argue that managing education organisations has shifted from a focus on the control of staff to the empowerment of staff. This strategy is more responsive to change and maximises organisational performance. They claim that women may be better suited to lead schools in the future than men.

Similarly Pedlar, Burgoyne and Boydell (1991) argued that organisations have to 'continuously transform themselves in response to the needs, wishes and aspirations of people, inside and outside' (p. 1). To achieve this they have to be constantly learning and reflecting. This is a similar idea to that of a commitment to continuous improvement found in Total Quality Management. They suggest that more 'feminine' values are needed, moving away from leadership through control of hierarchies and towards empowerment and network structures.

In education, however, the move to Local Management may have led to the erosion of collegiality and flexibility. Jenkins (1992) (quoting Weightman 1988) says that the professional culture of participation is being replaced by an inappropriate and out-of-date managerialism. These more competitive, entrepreneurial styles with more prescriptive approaches to the curriculum may be less attractive to women.

Is this an inevitable response to the new responsibilities, or merely a temporary phase while new, more appropriate and effective, management styles are developed? Al-Khalifa (1989) argues that the management of schools is seen as demanding male, hierarchical, skills. 'The association of masculinity, male authority and school leadership is pervasive in the life of the school' (p. 85). The Total Quality Management approach (West Burnham 1992, Sallis 1993), however, argues for a more flexible, flatter management structure and style.

Are things changing outside education?

McLoughlin (1992) argues that business has become more feminine in recent years, and that women have become more highly valued by their peers and their managers. She claims that a cultural shift has occurred in new service and financial industries: the top 200 British companies now have 29 female directors, in 1980 there was one.

Her interviews with successful business women showed a marked difference between older women and younger women. While older women were in favour of positive action, younger women were not: they regarded it as a perpetuation of their second class status. The younger women tended to be in supportive second relationships which valued each partner's career. These women felt more supported at home and at work than their older colleagues. She also reported that women were opting out of male-dominated corporate cultures by starting their own businesses. This is not supported by Coe (1992) in her survey of women members of the Institute of Management. In this study slightly more younger women were in employment rather than owning their own companies: 'It is possible to speculate that women may now be finding it marginally easier to pursue mainstream management careers rather than turning to setting up their own business.' (p. 7).

Are men changing?

Does the new man exist? Davidson and Cooper (1992) and McLoughlin (1992) suggest that he does but that he may be rather rare. Henwood, Rimmer and Wicks (1987) (quoted in Davidson and Cooper, p. 141) reported that '73 per cent of women in the UK do nearly all the housework.' Alban-Metcalfe and West (1991) also report that in families where both partners work most domestic tasks are done by women. The traditional attitudes held by men about women are drawn out in Shakeshaft's chapter in this book.

McLoughlin (1992) is rather more positive. She reports that younger men are changing and becoming less macho and more concerned with the quality of life. She suggests that the decline of traditional male employment has led to men valuing women's employment more highly. But her sample was small, and she commented on the fact that many of her interviewees had divorced their traditional first husbands, and remarried men who were happy with a more equal balance of power and responsibilities within the partnership.

Will the position of women in education get better or worse?

As discussed in the previous section, the new management demands resulting from the *1988 Education Reform Act* may have led to more managerial styles of management, while research on the management of non-educational organisations has led to more flexible approaches. It seems likely that women will be disadvantaged by the first approach and advantaged by the second.

Newly empowered governing bodies will have a major impact on women's careers (Waring 1992). Will they tend to appoint male headteachers to manage the new financial responsibilities of schools? If the governing body is predominantly male and middle-aged this may lead to the recent advances made by women being halted. While the Equal Opportunities Commission continues to provide training materials for governors, its implementation depends on governing bodies, who may have other priorities.

The diminishing role of LEAs may also lead to a decline in the concern for equal opportunities for teachers and pupils. Equal opportunities advisers are no longer employed in many authorities, and their contribution to INSET will be lost. There may, therefore, be less emphasis on equal opportunities in employment and in the curriculum. It has also been suggested (*Independent on Sunday* 14 February 1993) that the recession is leading commercial companies to place less emphasis on equal opportunities in employment.

Resources for professional development are now devolved to schools. This may lead to a decline in support for all management development and in particular to programmes for women as they may be seen as focusing on personal, rather than organisational, development.

Conclusions

> '. . . getting women into top jobs demands strategic planning: it does not just happen through goodwill or good intentions'. (Hansard Society Commission quoted in Davidson and Cooper 1992, p.171)

It is very difficult to predict the future for women in education management. More women have been obtaining senior posts in recent years, although they are still grossly under-represented. Whether this improvement will continue will depend on the interaction of a wide range of personal, professional and cultural influences.

We cannot rely on just one or two approaches to reducing the existing inequalities. There are many different ways of empowering women to enable them to make a new contribution to the management of schools. Many of the issues have been raised in this chapter and will be explored in more detail in later chapters.

Acknowledgement

Data for Tables 1.1 – 1.5 published with the permission of the Controller of Her Majesty's Stationery Office.

References

Aisenberg, N. and Harrington, M. (1988) *Women of Academe: Outsiders in the Sacred Grove* Amherst: University of Massachusetts Press.

Alban-Metcalfe, B. and West, M. (1991) 'Women managers' in Firth-Cozens, J. and West, M. (eds) *Women at Work* Milton Keynes: Open University Press.

Alimo-Metcalf, B. (1991) 'What a waste! Women in the National Health Service' *Women in Management Review and Abstracts* **6**, 5, 17–24.

Al-Khalifa, E. (1989) 'Management by halves: women teachers and school management' in De Lyon, H. and Widdowson Migniuolo, F. (eds) *Women Teachers: Issues and Experiences* Milton Keynes: Open University Press.

British Institute of Management (1992) *National Management Salary Survey* London: BIM.

Buckby, R. (1992) 'Governing bodies: 1988–1992' *Management in Education* **6**, 4, 5–6.

Caldwell, B. and Spinks (1992) *Leading the Self Managing School* Lewes: Falmer.

Coe, T. (1992) *The Key to the Men's Club: Opening the Doors to Women in Management* London: The Institute of Management.

Coward, R. (1992) *Our Treacherous Hearts: Why Women Let Men Get Their Own Way* London: Faber.

Cusack, B. (1992) Personal communication.

Davidson, M. and Cooper, C. (1992) *Shattering the Glass Ceiling: The Woman Manager* London: PCP.
Department of Education and Science (1988) *Statistics of Education: Schools 1988* London: DES.
Department of Education and Science (1989) *Statistics of Education: Schools 1989* London: DES.
Department of Education and Science (1990) *Statistics of Education: Schools 1990* London: DES.
Department of Education and Science (1991) *Statistics of Education: Schools 1991* London: DES.
Department of Education and Science (1992) *Statistics of Education: Teachers in Service in England and Wales, 1989 and 1990* London: DES.
Department for Education (1993) *School Teachers' Review Body: Second Report*, February 1993. London: HMSO.
Eagly, A., Karau, S.and Johnson, B. (1992) 'Gender and leadership style among school principals: a meta-analysis' *Educational Administration Quarterly* **28**, 1, 76–102.
Esp, D. (1993) *Competences for School Managers* London: Kogan Page.
Hansard Society Commission (1990) *Women at the Top* London: Hansard Society.
Henwood, M., Rimmer, L. and Wicks, M. (1987) *Inside the Family: Changing Roles of Men and Women* London: Family Policies and Study Centre.
Jenkins, H. (1992) *Getting It Right: A Handbook of Successful School Leadership* Oxford: Blackwell.
Marshall, J. (1984) *Women Managers: Travellers in a Male World* Chichester: Wiley.
McBurney, E. and Hough, J. (1989) 'Role perceptions of female deputy heads' *Educational Management and Administration* **17**, 3, 115–18.
McLoughlin, J. (1992) *Up and Running: Women in Business* London: Virago.
Migniuolo, F. (1992) *Teacher's Careers and Equal Oppportunities* Public Finance Foundation Conference, London, January 1992.
Naisbitt, J. and Aburdene, P. (1990) *Megatrends 2000* New York: William Morrow.
Ozga, J. (1993) *Women in Educational Management* Milton Keynes: Open University Press.
Pedler, M., Burgoyne, J.and Boydell, T. (1991) *The Learning Company: a Strategy for Sustainable Developmen* London: McGraw Hill.
Peters, T.and Waterman, R. (1982) *In Search of Excellence* New York: Harper Row.
Powney, J. and Weiner, G. (1991) *Outside the Norm: Equity and Management in Educational Institutions* London: South Bank Polytechnic.
Sallis, E. (1993) *Total Quality Management in Education* London: Kogan Page.
Schmuck, P. (1986) 'School management and administration: an analysis by gender' in Hoyle, E.and McMahon, A.(eds) *The World Yearbook of Education, 1986* London: Kogan Page.

Schon, D.A. (1971) *Beyond the Stable State* New York: Norton.

Sergiovanni, T. (1990) *Value-Added Leadership* San Diego: Harcourt Brace Janovich.

Spencer, A. (1987) 'Women in further and higher education management: forward and introduction' *Coombe Lodge Report* **20**, 3, 131–137.

Spencer, A. and Podmore, D. (1987) (eds) *In a Man's World: Essays on Women in Male-Dominated Professions* London: Tavistock.

Stainton, R. (1992) 'Coming, ready or not: attitudes to LMS' *Education 3–13* **20**, 1, 14–22.

Torrington, D. and Weightman, J. (1989) *The Reality of School Management* Oxford: Blackwell.

Travers, C. and Cooper, C. (1991) 'Stress and status in teaching: an investigtion of potential gender-related relationships' *Management Review and Abstracts* **6**, 4, 16–23.

Vinnicombe, S. (1987) 'What exactly are the differences in male and female working styles?' *Women in Management Review* **3**, 1, 13–21.

Waring, S. (1992) 'Women teachers' careers: do governors hold the key?' *Management in Education* **6**, 4, 14–16.

Weightman, J. (1988) Paper presented at the third BEMAS Research Conference, Cardiff, 1988.

Weightman, J. (1989) 'Women in management' *Educational Management and Administration* **17**, 3, 119–122.

West Burnham, J. (1992) *Managing Quality in Schools* London: Longman.

Whitehead, J. (1993) 'The head of department in teacher education' in Ozga, J. (ed.) *Women in Educational Management* Milton Keynes: Open University Press.

2 The development of women managers in education, or, how to talk about it

Anne Gold

I have been surprised by the difficulties, and sometimes strong feelings, aroused when I begin to talk about the part of my work which involves women in education management. I tried, initially, to select my audience when I spoke about it. Then I decided that it is such an important area for exploration that I should talk about it as much as possible. I often meet resistance, either in the form of intellectual obfuscation, or in a more raw emotive way. I recognise many of the forms that the resistance takes. They reproduce the sort of resistance women meet when trying to break into management in education. Sometimes, I am made to feel as though I lack intellectual rigour — I have not really understood the context for management; I have not read all the available literature and so on. Sometimes I am made to feel inept — I have not understood the available literature, and it should be explained more carefully to me so that I will understand. Sometimes it is made obvious to me that I am wasting valuable time, so the explanations will be presented to me another time. And worst of all, I am made to feel like an novice who is too lightweight to be afforded enough respect to be taken seriously.

But I come from many years' experience as a woman manager in education and I have spent several years working to develop other women managers, validated by our recent research (Ouston, Gold and Gosling 1992). Why am I being made to feel as though I am denied access to several bodies of knowledge? Why do I feel powerless so often in these exchanges? I have realised that my sense of exclusion comes from the difficulties entailed in engaging in other peoples' discourses. Ball (1990) explains the concept of 'Discourses' as identified by Foucault:

> Discourses are about what can be said and thought, but also about who can speak, when, and with what authority. Discourses embody meaning and social relationships, they constitute both subjectivity and power relations . . . Thus the possibilities for meaning and for definition, are pre-empted through the social and institutional position held by those who use them. (p. 2)

So, I have begun to think about how and why these difficulties are presented to me and what is my part in them. It seems to me that within my exploration, teaching and writing about this particular area of interest, I take several other explorations as read. In working within my own discourse, I ignore many others. Like stepping stones, taken for granted and hurried over to get to the other side, some of them are firmly embedded, obvious, and known by all travellers. Others are slippery, need to be negotiated with care, and sometimes need to be anchored more firmly. So the various discourses on my way to this one are treated differently by different people. Some of them are well-researched with large bodies of published writing, and others are under-explored. Some of them need more exploration by some people and not by others. For example, in a seminar I gave on this subject, a man suggested to me that radical feminists would not be comfortable with any notions of women managing, because management was disempowering. I could not engage in this discourse immediately. Initially, I thought that my inability to engage was because I was surprised by it. I certainly knew that I wanted to say that I believed that most feminists would be uncomfortable with disempowering styles of management, but enthusiastic about empowering styles of management, especially those that empowered women, or were predicated on more 'female' ways of working with people. But the very powerful and authoritative manner in which he 'explained' my apparently poor reasoning meant that I was denied entry to his discourse.

At the same seminar, other people, making no reference to gender in their discourse, wanted to articulate their ideas about management, quoting Ball (1990):

> Theories of management reflect the particular interests and needs of administrators . . . management empowers the manager and objectifies and subjects the managed. (p. 165)

Other people said that even 'empowering' management was a form of manipulation, even if in a more subtle form. Joe Winston (1992) gives a fascinating description of his 'management' of a piece of planning when he was a new headteacher, in which he originally thought that he had been a 'good manager', but later he understood that he had manipulated his staff into agreeing with him. On reflection, he realised that the manipulation had not been necessary. He did not need to work like that again because it was not as effective as his more reflective collegiate management style:

> I must conclude that the disparity between my theory and my practice was not inevitable; that a divided staff need not have led me down the road of managerial manipulation; and that the conscious, reflective, intentional action of praxis would appear to provide a more suitable model for action than would Machiavellian cleverness. (p. 146)

> Being *reflective* and being *effective* are not mutually exclusive states. The purpose of the above case study was to illuminate, not to find a quick-fix solution to a perceived problem. Understanding is bound to influence action, however. (p. 14)

I spend much of my time at the Management Development Centre encouraging senior managers in education to develop their own reflective collaborative styles of management and decision-making which are based on the understanding of the need to empower those who are managed so that they can enter into transformative dialogues about their work. I read about it, I write about it, I *do* it, but I could not talk about it during the seminar.

But I too am guilty of refusing to engage in other discourses. In my impatience to reach the discussion about the development of women managers in education, I may be taking too many discussions and explorations for granted. I think that in working on the development of women managers in education, there is a confluence of thinking and writing about the following issues:

- the position of women in our society;
- the position of girls in this education system;
- the position of women in teaching;
- women in management;
- management as empowerment;
- gender issues in management styles;
- management in education;
- management or leadership?
- managing this educational system;
- developing learning with experienced adult professionals;
- developing educational managers;
- encouraging women into education management.

And I am not always prepared to enter into detailed examinations of each of these discourses. I seem to have decided which ones are worth exploring, and which ones I shall ignore. I have subconsciously developed a hegemonic structure of discourses which determines when I will enter into the argument and when I will ignore it.

A very interesting example of the way one discourse can completely exclude another within my structure, so that there is not the opportunity to explore absolutely valid issues, is my reading of the work of Hodgkinson (1991). He examines educational leadership as a moral art, introducing such important notions as the place of education in society, the problems with leadership, and value theory and practice. But he does so, in 1991, in a book in which women are invisible, and in which the use of feminine pronouns are dismissed in the preface 'in the interests of clarity, emphasis, or literary merit'.

I realise that I, too, become entrapped in certain discourses as I find myself encountering difficulty with literature on education management if it does not refer to the issues that particularly affect women in management. I had to acknowledge to myself my discomfort in continuing with Hodgkinson's writing, and my sense that he had not taken into account enormously important other discourses. In understanding my difficulties, I could then pay attention to his argument, and could indeed benefit from it. But I felt a sense of loss for both of us.

I felt some of the same loss when reading Duignan and Macpherson (1992). They address aspects of race but not of gender. Does this mean that they have nothing to say to or about the woman in me? It certainly means that once again, I have to struggle to overcome my initial inclination not to 'listen' to them because I feel an almost physical exclusion from their discourse — if women are invisible, am I invisible? And the same old welling up of irritation made it difficult for me to read their writings with any receptivity. I now recognise in myself the same irritation that other people show me when I appear not to take into account the positions they bring to *my* discourse.

Is it possible to enter into an 'alien' discourse and colonise it, or even to co-exist with it? An example of this, of one strongly held set of educational values taking over another powerful set of values might be the way many schools have approached their entry into the marketplace. Initial abhorrence at being forced to sell themselves has given way to designing a persuasive package which can seduce a local community. Close examination of some of that packaging shows just how far the discourse of the marketplace can be colonised. The integrity of the school mission statement can be tested by the way notions such as equity and social justice are threaded through the publicity. What and who do the illustrations show? What access is there to languages other than English? And indeed, what style of English is used? What verbal and non-verbal allusions are there to gender? How are the staff introduced? What expectations are there of the achievements of the children? What is the value basis on which the young people are offered access to learning other than the National Curriculum? All these questions and many more can be used to explore the educational philosophy of a school through its packaging.

And many schools have taken the opportunity to embed their own discourses of the Left within an enforced discourse of the Right.

How far can we ignore a discourse and refuse to engage with it because it does not 'fit' our argument? The Government has certainly done this very successfully within education. Professional discourses of how children learn most effectively and what they should learn, of the inter-linking of social justice and education provision, of the most effective ways of managing learning within institutions have all been ignored. They have been dominated and subsumed under a 'common sense', populist, model of consumerism — we know what sort of education system we want to buy in order to produce the types of citizens necessary to the continuation of the Conservative model of society!

So perhaps I should sometimes colonise and sometimes ignore the different discourses that constrain me in my attempt to cross the stepping stones, and reach the other side, where the development of women educational managers is, to me, an unequivocal example of social justice.

Most liberal and radical educators would agree that the intended end product of an education system is to empower people to enter into dialogue about their lives in order to transform their position to one when conscious decisions can be made and followed through. In the most orthodox explorations of Marxist writers such as Freire, there is an understanding of educational organisations and those in them whose work it is to encourage the sort of work described above, that must encourage women, and black people, into positions where they can effect that transformation.

Paula Allman (1987), describes Freire's transformative dialogue as a group activity where 'participants undertake a critical analysis of their reality and formulate explanations capable of challenging the conventional ones'. If one of the aims of education and those managing it is to encourage transformative dialogue in both learners and teachers, then it is important that space is made for the necessary group activity. However, Allman makes it clear that dialogue is not an easy or automatic activity:

> A group cannot enter into dialogue without considering how it challenges forms of communication such as discussion. Even with careful consideration, it's not likely that participants will commit themselves to the process of dialogue unless . . . they share a desire to learn to relate to one another in ways which will produce caring, trust and a willingness to question the knowledge they already possess, i.e. to be critical and curious. (p. 221)

This particular understanding of group activity is why my central premise is the necessity for encouraging and developing more women managers in education. The type of work involved in dialogue must take into account the power balance within the group. At least some members of the group must have an understanding of the societal oppressions the group is seeking to address, so that they are not reproduced, unresolved, within the group:

> Dialogue is intended to be a way of relating, one to another, the effect of which is radical because it produces the development of trust, care, collaboration and commitment amongst the participants rather than competition and individualism. (Allman, p. 223)

In schools, half the people engaged in dialogue are girls and women. The power relations in the world-to-be-transformed must not be so transferred into the group activity that the necessary transformation cannot take place. Those who have been oppressed by those power relations, who have understood them, and who may have come some way to transforming them for themselves are most able to help other girls and women in dialogue. So, women must be present within the group activity, not merely as representatives, but actively involved. The supreme importance, then, of the existence of 'successful' women managers in schools as role models for girls as examples of success, and as role models for boys as examples of different ways of managing, becomes clear.

If dialogue, in Freire's terms, is a way of transforming lives, then space must be made to encourage it within educational organisations. Many teachers already work this way, asking questions which challenge 'common sense' explanations about the lives of the learners they work with. The National Curriculum restricts the time for this in-school dialogue. Managers have to help teachers interpret the National Curriculum in a way that still allows for dialogue.

References

Allman, P. (1987), 'Paulo Freire's education approach: a struggle for meaning' in Allen, Bastiani, Martin and Richards (eds) *Community Education* Milton Keynes: Open University Press.

Ball, S. (ed.) (1990) *Foucault and Education* London: Routledge.

Duignan, P.A. and Macpherson, R.J.S. (eds) (1992) *Educative Leadership* London: Falmer Press.

Hodgkinson, C. (1991) *Educational Leadership: The Moral Art* New York: State University of New York Press.

Ouston, J. Gold, A and Gosling, P. (1992) *The Development of Managers in Education* Paper given at the BEMAS Research Conference, Nottingham, Easter 1992.

Winston, J. (1992) 'The school management plan: a case study in the ethics of school management' *Teacher Development* **1**, 3, October.

3 Women in educational management: a review of research in Britain

Valerie Hall

Introduction

Compared to the United States, research on women in educational management in Britain is still in its infancy. Ask Shakeshaft's (1989) question, 'Does this research or theory include or explain the experiences of women?' of educational administration in Britain and the answer is a resounding no. The sterility of the field is well illustrated in Hough's (1986) review of a leading professional journal (*Educational Management and Administration*). He found it to be as androcentric as its counterparts in the United States had been found to be. He defines androcentrism as viewing the world and shaping reality through a male lens. According to this view the experiences of men and women educators are assumed to be the same. As a result research on males is deemed appropriate for generalising to the female experience. Of the 140 articles analysed by Hough, only five or six indicated strong gender awareness and thoroughly explored gender related issues. Eighty eight per cent had male authors, 10 per cent female and 2 per cent joint. Although he detected a trend towards more articles showing improved awareness of gender issues, the subsequent five years' issues show 70 per cent still to have male authors only and relatively few address gender issues.

The absence of women authors reflects, no doubt, the relative absence of women from academic life or their more humble positions in the research hierarchy. Lyon and West (1992) show their under-representation in polytechnics and universities and their concentration in the lower ranks of both hierarchies. While questioning the definition of productivity being used to judge academic output, the authors acknowledge the effects of a multitude of factors combining to create the glass ceiling through which it is so hard for women to penetrate and which, potentially, limits their publication rate. Even Hough's article, written as sole author, ends by acknowledging a woman colleague for having carried out all of the empirical work. She is not included however as a joint author, a significant omission in a research climate in which publications count for everything. Moreover, even if male researchers and authors dominate the publications lists, they have a choice about demonstrating gender awareness at each stage of the research project.

The failure to include gender issues in discussions of educational management extends well beyond the journal pages. Analyses of school leadership in Britain from 1986 on fail to integrate gender as a relevant concept. When it is considered (e.g. Hall *et al.* 1986, Weindling and Earley 1987, Torrington and Weightman 1987) it is an aside rather than a significant contribution to a conceptualisation of school leadership. For example, Jenkins' (1991) handbook for successful school leadership is based on 'useful theoretical perspectives' but includes gender as a one page discussion of the extent to which secondary schools constitute predominantly masculine environments. One of his prescriptions for 'getting it right' represents, he claims, 'the feminine side':

> School leaders have neglected to display the 'feminine' qualities of caring, tolerance, warmth and valuing. As a result school staff feel uncared for and undervalued. Leaders should make each member of staff's future and development a prime concern.

The association of one set of qualities with 'masculine' or 'feminine' remains unquestioned and is treated as unproblematic. Even Jones (1987), writing as a successful senior women educator, gives no more than a passing reference to gender as a factor in leadership of tomorrow's schools. In most cases a plea for additional research is made, but gender continues to be treated as a separate issue rather than a powerful tool for restructuring conceptualisations of school life and leadership.

The relatively small number of research reports that form the main focus of this chapter demonstrate that discussions of the implications of gender for an understanding of management in schools have increased but offer little empirical data in support of the arguments. Most discussions remain at the level of hypotheses, particularly where they relate to women's styles of management and experience of managing schools. A study by Acker (1992) of a single school attempts to show how gender, as a variable, permeates institutional life, the gender overlay of educational institutions, the often unintentional behaviours and practices which perpetuate gender based employment patterns. It is impossible to generalise from this about the extent to which gender can be said to permeate life in all schools, though it raises an agenda for further research. Other research studies in this area in Britain are more firmly rooted in empirical data when they are discussing women's careers in teaching and how they differ from men's. The dearth of evidence is highlighted by the fact that the only recent review of research into women and school management (Riches 1989) cites only two empirical studies, both by the same author (Evetts 1986, 1989). The rest of the review is discursive and relies heavily on the American research.

The focus of this chapter is on research published since 1980. Most of it relates to women in school management, with only a few references to women in further and higher education. Studies fall mainly into two categories. The first re-examines the concept of career (including selection, promotion and training) to take account of women's experiences. What, for example, are the psychological and institutional factors that deter women from assuming positions of school leadership? The second looks for evidence of a typical female style of management and raises questions about the equation of management with men. Are there sex differences in the performance of leadership? Do women bring something different to the role of leader compared to men?

Overall the research is mainly descriptive and based on small samples. Described in terms of Schmuck's (1987) developmental model to trace thinking about gender as a relevant concept in educational administration, it is very much at stage four, that is women are seen as oppressed by institutional processes which treat them differently. The 'New Scholarship' which constitutes Schmuck's fifth stage (in which gender is a primary area of concentration) is only just emerging from the wings. As a result much of the research that has been done in Britain is compensatory and looks at women who have achieved roles primarily held by men. Exceptions are recent work by Evetts 1990, Powney and Weiner 1991, Acker 1992, all of whom reject the notion of men as the norm and attempt to respond to Schmuck's (1987) exhortation:

> To understand the phenomenon of leadership we need concepts that do not presume the male experience as universal and speaks to all humanity. Women need to be included as objects and subjects of study in leadership and we need to investigate how our concepts of leadership have been formed by the blinding assumption that leader means male.

Together with Shakeshaft, Schmuck has set the agenda for research into gender and educational administration in both the United States and Britain. Both review a range of theories purporting to explain the under-representation of women in senior educational posts. Shakeshaft (1989) holds firmly to the view that the most satisfactory model is the one which sees male dominance leading to conditions that keep women from advancing into positions of power and prestige. But, as she points out, the same data can be explained in a variety of ways. Ball (1987) and Byrne-Whyte (1987) demonstrate this with their different theoretical perspectives on evidence of women's under-representation in management posts in schools in Britain. In spite of attempting to incorporate a gender dimension into his analysis of the micropolitics of schools, Ball's discussion is restricted to a reiteration of the organisational constraints argument (Schmuck 1986) and the identification of group affiliation as a collective response to something (unequal promotion opportunities) that is not otherwise defined as a valid concern. His profiles of 'women who make it' are drawn mainly from the United States or outside education. Byrne-Whyte attempts a four part typology of women's attitudes to promotion, influenced first by organisational and work culture structures that accept or reject women and second, by the character of women's relationships with their male partner. Having explored the 'moral superiority' view (that women prefer to avoid competition, value co-operative social and working relationships and find hierarchical structures antipathetical), she concludes that women's under-representation at senior levels is a consequence of their position in the workforce which leads to the perception that they are not suited to leadership roles. This in turn is combined with variations in their personal relationships which influence the degree of support available to them in furthering their careers. She is critical of the tendency of most explanations to assume women to be a homogeneous group, thereby failing to do justice to 'the variety of human relationships and responses among members of the same sex to personal and professional demands' (p.181). Acker's (1980) feminist analysis of women in academic life points to the tendency to identify just one specifically sociological variable (family) relating to women academics to explain their under-representation at senior levels of the academic hierarchy. In her view it combines with a deficit model of women which operates to make it impossible for them to be acceptable or even visible within the androcentric culture of academia.

Outside education, Marshall's (1984) research on women managers as travellers in a male world has contributed significantly to extending the theoretical boundaries. Having considered and rejected a purely 'reformist' viewpoint (in which women are encouraged to aspire to a management world defined in male terms) and a purely 'radical' perspective (all men are oppressors) she develops a third theoretical position that culls from both. This is based on the principles of 'agency' and 'communion' as strategies for dealing with uncertainty. She distinguishes these two orientations in terms of their aims and characteristics. Agentic principles relate to control and independence with an emphasis on achieving change and mastery through 'doing'. Communion approaches, in contrast, value union and interdependence, adaptiveness and 'being'. Application of these principles to management leads her to redefine it in terms of the integration of the two, neither the exclusive property of either men or women. While many of her findings about women's exclusion from the masculine world of management echo the school research, the question remains whether the organisational cultures which are the focus of her study (retail and publishing) are similar enough to education to make comparisons feasible and useful.

Women teachers' careers

Setting the agenda

If women were promoted in proportion to their numbers in the teaching workforce and assuming they are no less capable than men, they would hold at least 60 per cent of senior posts in schools and colleges, instead of the minority position they hold now. Only in LEAs has there been a notable increase in the number of women senior managers. In 1985 there were no women chief education officers. In 1990 there were 12 out of 116 and more being appointed. While this might reflect equal opportunities policies coming to fruition (in a way that has not been evident in other areas of education) it may equally reflect the envisaged demise of LEAs, making them a less attractive career proposition for men. If this is the case, the concomitant lowering of status means that it is more likely that women will be considered for senior posts and the risk of appointing one more easily taken. There is an interesting parallel in elementary schools in the United States where, Fullan (1991) notes but does not seek to explain, the fact that fewer men are entering or heading such schools at a time when they are seen increasingly as undesirable workplaces.

As well as being under-represented at senior level, women's promotion position has deteriorated over the past 20 years. During the 1980s explanations of their differential position proliferated, with an increasing focus on how their experience of career differed from that of men. This interest paralleled the shift of research focus into teachers' careers from large scale surveys such as Hilsum and Start's (1974) to life history accounts such as Sikes *et al.* (1985). Both strands were androcentric in that they failed to question the concept of career in the light of women's experiences although both also referred to differences in promotion opportunities. Sikes *et al.*'s life history approach opened up the way for questioning definitions of career which assume 'a succession of related jobs, arranged in a hierarchy of prestige through which persons move in an ordered, predictable sequence' (p.127). They postulated for both men and women an alternative version of career which is subjective, takes a whole life view and is concerned with a teacher's on-going development and identity.

Acker (1989), in contrast, makes gender the central theme of her book on teachers' careers. She sees her task to map the variations in promotions, subjects taught, administrative responsibilities and daily experience. In this way she aims to rectify a situation in which:

> . . . many possible questions about teachers' careers and experiences have not yet been answered or even asked, because the dominant model has limited the scope of our collective imagination. (p.18)

One example demonstrates well how the focus of attention has shifted. Hilsum and Start's 1974 study found a strikingly low promotion orientation among women teachers, based on their evidence that only 16 per cent of women teachers interviewed wanted headships compared to 50 per cent of men. Apart from their very small interview sample (only 69 women and 71 men) they fail to question why this might be so. In 1980, a National Union of Teachers' study of promotion and the woman teacher analysed 2,829 returns from women teachers and concluded that:

> Female teachers, both married and single, show a high degree of career orientation and would welcome the challenge and opportunity of promotion. (p.34)

In common with Davidson (1985) they scotched a whole range of myths about women teachers which previous research had failed to challenge.

In the United States Shakeshaft (1989) took the debate about women teachers' motivation still further by questioning explanations of women managers' behaviour based on male paradigms of leadership and effectiveness. In her view, given the constraints on women's careers, their 'promotion orientation' is bound to emerge as lower if it is interpreted within this paradigm. The concepts need to be redefined if they are accurately to reflect women's experiences. Martini *et al.* (1984) carried out a comparative study of men and women teachers in ILEA to provide an explanation of their different application rates and attitudes to promotion. The authors concluded that women teachers have a different rather than lower orientation to promotion. Women weigh more carefully the benefits of their present job against what promotion might bring and are more discriminating in their applications (p.8).

Grant (1989) set out to celebrate the success of women who had achieved deputy headship in comprehensive schools. Her interviews with 38 women deputy heads in one LEA led her to question the concept of aspiration levels as a static and objective measure of career intentions, as based on male experiences (p.41). Her proposal for an alternative model of 'career' contrasts with the continuing use of an androcentric model in Spencer *et al.*'s (1987) report of interviews with six women in senior positions in further and higher education. They view their respondents' careers from a perspective which highlights the masculine environment of further and higher education and how women adapt in order to succeed.

Generally during the 1980s the focus has shifted from measuring women's career performance alongside men's in teaching to interpreting women teachers' careers within a new paradigm that has women rather than men as its starting point. This shift is best exemplified in the work of Evetts (1990) whose analysis of women in primary teaching supports an alternative model of career. Her interviews with 25 primary headteachers focus on how individuals have constructed and developed their careers and what having a career means to the individuals involved. She describes primary women teachers' careers as characterised by strategic compromises to negotiate the constraints and make use of the occupational advantages of teaching. She uses the concepts of 'local primary teaching labour markets' and 'occupational culture' as relevant to explanations of women's promotion prospects in primary schools. The concepts are relatively unexplored in research using a gender perspective at secondary school level apart from a small scale study by Cunnison (1985) that identifies the male dominated culture of the secondary school as an obstacle to women's promotion. In Evetts' view, the combination of the characteristics of the occupational culture of teaching and processes that encourage and discourage teachers from seeking promotion combine with individual teachers' subjective attempts to construct their careers.

The new research agenda for women's promotion experiences in teaching is effectively summarised and extended in Al-Khalifa's (1989) assertion of a convergence of masculinity and management roles. In common with Shakeshaft she discerns an association between theories of organisational leadership and masculinity which deter women from identifying with the role of manager. Alternative models of career need to be accompanied by a reconceptualisation of management to include women's experience and interpretation (p. 92). At this stage of limited research the proposition remains unsupported by empirical evidence.

Research that has been carried out into women teachers' career and promotion patterns falls into two strands. On the one hand are small and large scale surveys, either exclusively questionnaire or combining interviews and questionnaires (NUT 1980, ILEA 1984, AMMA 1985, Davidson 1985, Hunter 1987, Earley and Weindling 1988, Weightman 1989, AUT 1989, Jones 1990). Both the Earley and Weindling and Weightman accounts are based on larger surveys of school managers (Weindling and Earley 1987 and Torrington and Weightman 1987) in which women as managers was not taken as a specific focus for study. Conclusions about their different career paths and experiences are extrapolated rather than integrated with the main substance of the report. The same is true of Morgan *et al.*'s (1983) study of the selection of secondary heads which includes a section on the experiences of women applying for headship. Evetts' (1991) follow up study also includes women rather than making them the exclusive focus. All the others have women teachers as their central focus but are mainly descriptive and atheoretical, aiming to paint a picture of where women are in teaching compared to men.

The other strand of research uses structured and semi-structured interviews, including the collection of life history accounts, with small samples of women teachers (Williams 1981, Spencer *et al.* 1987, Grant 1989, Evetts 1991, Powney and Weiner 1991). The interview method allows in-depth exploration of women teachers' own perceptions of their promotion experiences, choices and strategies within the constraints imposed by the historical, social and occupational structures that shape their lives. Ozga (1992) presents a range of interesting accounts by women who are senior managers in education but they are accounts only, not based on research nor analysed and interpreted. Powney and Weiner's study includes men and women since their interest is in the strategies used and obstacles faced by women and black managers in educational institutions.

All these studies share a concern to depict and offer explanations for women's position in education management. The surveys are mainly descriptive and atheoretical, stimulated in some cases by the professional association's concern to improve women's status in the profession. Explanations of women's under-representation are mainly in terms of organisational constraints, demonstrated particularly in the barriers to promotion constituted by current arrangements for selection, re-entry and management development. A fourth barrier emerges in some of these studies as an important component of explanations of women in education management; the conceptualisation of management as masculine and schools, particularly secondary schools, as representing masculine cultures.

In contrast, the studies based on interview data attempt to extend the theoretical boundaries by questioning traditional concepts of career, motivation and labour markets. What is not apparent in the research literature of the last decade are the previously popular 'deficiency' explanations of women's under-representation. These are summarised in Davidson's (1985) 'unfriendly myths about women teachers'; they contribute less than men, want promotion less, are less well qualified, have less experience, are less committed to the job, are less respected as teachers by pupils. All the studies cited above provide evidence that refutes one or more of these myths and points to alternative explanations of women's position in educational management.

The empirical studies challenge the 'unfriendly myths' mainly by identifying the organisational barriers to promotion. They show that getting selected constitutes a primary obstacle, if only because women's different conceptions of career are not yet understood by the majority of selectors who judge them in typically androcentric ways. Both Evetts (1991) and Grant (1989) show the importance of career encouragement and sponsorship, not always available to women in systems dominated by male preferment. Those women candidates for promotion who felt they were compared unfavourably in interviews to male norms (Grant 1989, p.46) would find their fears confirmed in Morgan *et al.*'s (1983) POST Project on selection for secondary headship. At a time when LEAs had a main responsibility for selecting heads, the POST Project showed the process skewed by the predominance of men among education officers. Although the 1988 *Education Act* has shifted that power to governors there is now an even greater concern that, in the absence of explicit criteria, lay selectors may rely still more heavily on 'unfriendly myths' to guide their choice. For example, Mortimore and Mortimore (1991) conclude from the accounts of eight secondary heads that:

> The traditional image of a white, middle class headmaster is still widely held, despite the increasing numbers of highly effective headteachers who are women or who are members of black and ethnic minority communities. (p.167)

Hunter's (1987) sample reported questions about childcare, marriage plans and family planning still being asked in spite of complaints procedures.

Morgan *et al.* found that although women applied in smaller numbers (which in no way reflected their proportion of the whole teaching force) they proportionately stood the same chance of succeeding as male applicants. Men however, were more likely to get headships of girls' schools than women of boys' schools. This situation continues particularly in the independent sector where women are barred from membership of the Headmasters' Conference but men can become heads of independent girls' schools. POST found that to be considered seriously alongside men, women candidates had to be tough (but not too tough) and overcome a whole range of stereotypes in selectors' minds of women in positions of authority. Evetts' (1991) interviews in 1990 with ten men and ten women headteachers found that gender differences in the achievement of headship posts continued to be very large in spite of the claimed objectives of both LEAs and teacher unions in the equal opportunities policies. She attributes changes in the process of selection to changing perceptions of the headship role. Although the selection processes currently reflect some of POST's recommendations regarding more systematic and 'fair' selection, the changes in the headship role may result in even less women applying or in being successful when measured against a model of headship that reflects Marshall's 'agentic' principles (competitive, efficient, task-centred) rather than 'communion'.

Martini *et al.* (1984) looked particularly at possible sex discrimination in teaching appointments at all levels. They found that more women thought they might be discriminated against in selection than reported experiencing it and commented on the difficulties of actually establishing whether negative discrimination has occurred. A related methodological issue is noted by Spencer *et al.* when interviewing women who had been successful in further and higher education. The fact that none of their respondents reported having experienced discrimination led them to the rather surprising conclusion that 'successful women are unlikely to have encountered discrimination'. This ignores the subtle ways (particularly since equal opportunities legislation) in which it continues to operate and the negative consequences on application rates of women's perceptions that it might occur. As Grant (1989) concludes:

> In a promotional system which does not make use of a formal method of career appraisal or generally make explicit the criteria by which appointees are selected, the way in which male preferment operates can only be guessed at.

She gives as an example those 'successful' women in her sample who valued classroom competency more than professional activities outside school in the early stages of their careers, a choice not necessarily also valued by promoters. Her findings lead her to advocate clear identification of promotion criteria and regular career reviews to support women's promotion prospects. Similarly Morgan *et al.* concluded that 'differential treatment of women is one of the strongest arguments for validated selection exercises' (p.77).

The growing popularity of assessment centres for educational managers reflects a move in the direction of the POST recommendations but these involve mainly senior managers. Research suggests that much of the discrimination occurs at the earlier stages of a teacher's career, in job placement, the provision of opportunities for management development and in the distribution of scale posts.

Inequities in job placement are most likely to occur at the point of women's re-entry into teaching, where this has constituted a break in their career. Here researchers differ in their conclusions. Both Trown and Needham (1981) and Grant (1989) conclude that re-entry problems constitute in women's eyes a considerable barrier to advancement. The operation of an age-related career structure and limited childcare arrangements mean that the potential benefits of legitimate maternity leave are undermined. While recognising the problem, the experiences of Evetts' (1990) career history headteachers lead her to question the appropriateness of describing women teachers as having broken or interrupted careers. She found that stopping work to have a family was part of many women teachers' career strategies, adding positively not negatively to their personal and professional development.

The increasing emphasis of institutional staff development programmes on meeting whole school rather than individual teacher career needs could have negative repercussions for women who are less likely to be in posts defined as 'management'. A number of studies point to inequities in the allocation of scale points that disadvantage women in seeking promotion. Where Hilsum and Start attributed differential distribution to the lower application rate of women at all levels, more recent explanations are located in gender influences on the status given to subjects. Spencer *et al.* (1987) describe further and higher education as labour markets internally segregated by gender. As a result promotion goes mainly to those in 'men's' subjects, whereas male entrants into female areas have meteoric rises. Evetts' (1990) comparative analysis of changes in the distribution of scale points between 1966 and 1987 showed a continuing trend for women to occupy the lower ranks, even when the primary sector was expanding.

Weightman (1989) describes the MOSS study of 24 secondary schools which found not only that fewer women than men were in posts of responsibility but also that women had to do more for less by having a dual role or accepting a lower grading of similar work. As a result of their high profile and straightforward jobs men were clearly seen as managers doing management work. In contrast the complex, cross-school jobs typically performed by women obscured rather than highlighted their management responsibilities. Martini *et al.* (1985) and Hunter (1987) also found that men tended to have higher grades than women for posts of the same description.

Decisions about who shall have development opportunities will be influenced by senior managers' (usually men) perceptions of individual teacher potential. Martini *et al.* (1984) found that more women reported that they had been refused permission to attend courses. The diversion of INSET budgets to schools removes one area of development that has been advocated as crucial if women are to overcome barriers to promotion: that of single sex training. There is, however, no research on the relative advantages of single and mixed training experiences for men and women's development as managers in schools. The choice depends on assumptions about the development needs of each group, which in turn depend on how management and management roles are defined. Appraisal offers further opportunities for identifying and meeting women teachers' development needs, but only if some of its inherent problems are confronted. Research on appraisal reported by Turner and Clift (1988) found evidence of gender stereotyping. Men but not women were encouraged to assert themselves and further their careers though some women who were not career ambitious were sometimes encouraged to be. Experience outside education suggests that male appraisers may be afraid to give negative feedback to women appraisees and by being over protective fail to enhance their development. Women are also often excluded from mentoring systems either because there are no women in influential positions who might act as mentors or because, as Kanter (1977) suggests, men do not identify with women and so fail to mentor and sponsor them. These inequities can only be redressed when more women enter senior management posts and have the power to influence development opportunities within the school.

At the start of the decade Williams (1981) found that in spite of the 1975 *Sex Discrimination Act*, women deputies were still most likely to be given traditional 'caring' tasks rather than, for example, curriculum responsibilities. Davidson's (1985) study confirmed the trend with women deputies being given jobs such as girls' welfare and lost property that did not constitute appropriate training for headship. Men dominated the Maths and Science head of department posts. More recently studies by McBurney and Hough (1989) and Wallace and Hall (1993) show that the creation of senior management teams in secondary schools has contributed to fewer women being confined to stereotyped roles in comparison with a decade ago. McBurney and Hough's interviews with ten female deputies revealed none to have followed an exclusively pastoral route although eight had held pastoral middle management posts. Only one had mainly pastoral duties as a deputy. They conclude that:

> An advertisement highlighting the importance of personality and individual strengths may be indicative of a very low level of stereotyping within the school. (p.117)

Similarly Wallace and Hall found that the decision to adopt a team approach to managing a secondary school was accompanied by a belief in allocating responsibilities according to the particular strengths of individuals and not gender stereotypes.

Women's approaches to management

Research as opposed to informed opinion on how women behave as managers in education lags behind that in the United States. There, research on women as school leaders is being linked to studies of school effectiveness and the claim made that 'as a group women are more likely to evidence behaviour associated with effective leadership' (Fullan 1991). The links remain hypothetical, not proven. A similar baseline for linking women's management styles to effective schools is missing in Britain. A recent study of the perceived characteristics of effectively managed schools (Bolam *et al.* 1993) used a sample of both men and women heads but deliberately obscured gender distinctions by altering the gender of teachers referred to on a random basis. This makes it impossible to associate with men or women the leadership styles identified as effective. In the absence of hard data this review of research can only point to the debate where it has been raised, outline the main issues and suggest directions for further investigation.

A useful starting point for reviewing the debate is Al-Khalifa and Migniuolos (1990) discussion of the identification of management in schools with masculinity. In their view:

> The association of masculinity, male authority and school leadership is pervasive in the life of the school.

Management is seen as technicist, requiring rational problem solving techniques, strong task direction and detachment. The same perspective emerges in Lyon and West's (1992) review of research on women academics and the variability of the extent to which they are willing to engage in and compete within the androcentric culture of the university. They comment on women academics' apparent unwillingness to conform to the meritocratic ethos of university life. They interpret this as a resistance to 'a discourse of rationality' that characterises the 'hegemonic male culture of academia'. In both these instances, women's attitudes to promotion and becoming managers are seen as shaped by the association they make between management and masculinity. Though the research evidence supporting the validity of the association is lacking, Marshall's study also shows it to be a powerful influence on women's career strategies and how they behave as managers.

Decisions about selecting and developing women for management posts can also be seen to be influenced by judgements about the extent to which they are seen as capable of meeting a masculine conception of its demands. Even if, as was suggested earlier, women managers in schools are less likely to be placed in sex stereotyped roles the association of management and masculinity continues. For example, Wallace and Hall's (1993) study of senior management teams in secondary schools shows that the decision to bring a woman on to the team was in most cases associated with a recognition of the need to have someone specifically responsible for staff development, an area of school management with a heavy emphasis on interpersonal skills. This was combined with a concern on all the teams about the under-representation of women in their membership. Stereotypical definitions of leadership in terms of masculine traits and behaviours are common, particularly in a climate of educational reform that stresses competition rather than collaboration. In this respect the arrival of management can be seen as having transformed the predominantly female world of school teaching (Miller 1992) into the more masculine one of school management. Evetts' (1990) postscript to her study of women primary teachers questions the potential effects of the 'new managerialism' on the qualities sought in primary heads of the future:

> The new managerialism seems to give prominence to qualities such as efficiency, accountability, ambition, striving and competition. At the same time qualities such as caring, nurturing, loyalty and co-operation are difficult to measure and hence difficult to reward. Yet these are the qualities that have made primary teaching and promotion in primary teaching attractive to many women.

Evetts' conclusions arise out of her life history research interviews. Al-Khalifa's are the result of wide experience of working with women teachers with management responsibilities. Neither would claim that their assumptions about what women bring to their performance as managers are based on observation of how they actually behave. There is no firm research base to support empirically the association of one set of qualities (such as detachment, task directiveness and rationality) with men or women. For example, the tension between the competencies required by heads and principals to support collaboration and those needed if their schools are to compete successfully may be as acute for men as they are for women. Al-Khalifa's association of masculinity and management is also questionable in the light of the experience of firms in the non-educational sector of the kinds of strategies they judge as most likely to lead to effectiveness. The concept of the 'androgynous manager' arises from the recognition of the need to manage both task and people and to combine instrumental and expressive behaviours. Sargent (1983) makes a case for the androgynous manager based on qualities which should be available to everyone, regardless of gender. The problem is in the association of one set of behaviours with men and the other with women as a result of different socialisation.

Life history research confirms that women's different life experiences will influence their performance as managers. However, as Jayne (1989) points out, there is no documentation of how women headteachers lead schools which might support or refute the hypothesis that their different life experience in a patriarchal society might lead to a different enactment of headship. Research data is needed of the characteristics women managers demonstrate in post and whether these are exclusive to women and congruent or incongruent with effective management. The possibly false equation of management with masculinity may be a factor in discouraging women from applying for management posts. However, once they have achieved management roles, they are managing. Then, management can be defined in terms of how they are doing it, not according to a pre-determined model which they may or may not fit.

How men and women behave as managers in schools is a result of what they bring to the job and a response to what others expect of them. Marshall's (1984) research into women managers outside education led her to the conclusion that:

> Women bring their femaleness with its connotations and status in society with them when they enter organizations. (p.4)

Her sample of 36 women managers in publishing and retail businesses was consistent in describing a core style that builds upon the qualities and advantages they have as a result of being women. At the same time they acknowledged their style as demonstrating both personal preference and a response to sex role stereotypes as well as the need at times to take responsibility for the disturbance their presence caused in predominantly masculine working environments.

Both Al-Khalifa in education and Marshall outside it conclude that the result of the identification of masculinity with management is a reluctance on the part of many women to move into the management role. They need confidence to apply and, if they are successful, to develop and use a style that may be continuously challenged as a result of sex stereotyping and unease about women in the leadership role, particularly if they have taken over from a man. Although Weindling and Earley's (1987) study looked at the early years of headship it did not use the opportunity to discover whether women's experiences were influenced by whether they followed a man or woman head. They found no differences in the amount of professional support received by men and women in the early years of headship but did not comment on how, for example, women secondary heads experienced their minority situation in heads' groups or working with governors with stereotyped expectations of headship behaviour.

David (1989) documents in detail her initial difficulties on moving to a head of department role in a polytechnic setting accustomed to men's style of leadership. Rejecting the 'business as usual' approach as sexist, she sought a personal style that allowed her to manage on her own terms and not within a white male paradigm. Similarly Powney and Weiner (1991) found personal self-confidence one of the keys to their sample of women and black managers in education becoming and remaining managers on their own terms.

What, then, are the qualities and skills associated with women managers in schools? What evidence is available to support the claim that women behave differently from men as managers in educational settings? Most of the studies use a comparative focus, that is they look at differences between men and women rather than what characterises women specifically. The problem with comparative studies is that they can encourage androcentric views by continuing to use a male concept definition of leadership. In contrast, studies (for example Evetts 1990 and Acker 1992) which start from the female world of administration, have as their focus how women perform, not how they are different from men, they assume the differences between women to be as important as the differences between women and men.

In the last five years the debate about management styles in education has shifted significantly, to bring into question the appropriate qualities for school leadership and the extent to which they challenge traditionally 'masculine' approaches (for example, Gray 1987, Acker 1992). Some comparative studies and discussions since 1980 of how men and women perform in school management hint at differences but the empirical base is thin (Cunnison 1985, Johnston 1986, Weightman 1989, Jayne 1989, Jones 1990, Powney and Weiner 1991). They are all based on questionnaires or interviews not observation. Apart from Acker's (1992) ethnographic study of one primary school, the first observational study of women in school management with a specific focus on gender is the one currently being conducted by the National Development Centre for School Management and Policy at the University of Bristol. This study combines in-depth interviews with focused observation over eighteen months of a small sample of women primary and secondary heads. It aims to test the tentative claims about women as school managers that have emerged from studies in the last ten years.

Cunnison's (1985) ethnographic account of what she called 'new career women' in one senior high school highlighted the strategies they adopted to cope with the heavily masculine ethos of the working environment. Ambitious for promotion, they sought ways of scotching the myth of 'family first' (by minimising references to domestic concerns); and strove to demonstrate continual competence. The problem with the second strategy was that it resulted at times in their personalities and femininity being called into question. Since their ambitiousness was not accompanied by a commitment to feminism, this was a potentially threatening and isolating outcome. As an example of the use of alternative strategies used by women Cunnison describes women teachers' approach to disciplining pupils more used to the literally heavy handed approach of their male colleagues. As a result of recognising the limitations of their physical strength or a reluctance to use coercive power, they were more likely to call on quick thinking, cunning, charm, good timing or moral authority to deal with the situation.

Byrne-Whyte (1987) refers to claims of women's preference for avoiding competition and conflict as the 'moral superiority view'. This neo-feminist perspective suggests innate differences in women and men. By implication, and if management is equated with masculinity, women can only succeed in management if they adapt to the masculine culture (thereby denying their 'natural' characteristics) or by getting into positions of power and changing structures from within. Two of Cunnison's sample demonstrated this approach when they questioned the necessity for such rigid hierarchical management structures. Ball (1987) also sees women teachers as marginalised unless they behave like men. Like Cunnison, he describes the difficulties of men teachers in accepting a woman's perspective as valuable or informative in its own right and the paranoia and hostility produced among men by a more assertive feminist perspective. He cites the example of the attempts by an all-woman English department to control the definition of what counts as school English, by establishing their right to participate in the formal processes of institutional decision-making and to speak out in micropolitical contexts. The resulting taunts and jibes from male colleagues are interpreted by Ball (from within his micropolitical framework) as a result of perception of feminism as a threat to their masculinity and as an attempt to redefine the political ethos of the school (p.76).

Senior women in further and higher education also reported problems of coping with a mainly male peer group and its expectations of them to be 'one of the boys' (Spencer *et al.*, 1987). The characteristics needed to be successful were stereotyped as masculine. As a result, the women felt that the more they conformed to the 'masculine' stereotype and were also perceived by their male peers to be successful, they were also seen as 'unfeminine' and 'unnatural' women.

These interpretations of women's situation in educational institutions support a view of the dominance of a masculine ethos in shaping work opportunities. Studies of primary schools are less likely to show women teachers as marginalised (e.g. Nias *et al.*, 1989). They also tend to take gender for granted rather than something to be questioned. Gray's (1987) experience with men primary headteachers and Alexander's (1989) analysis of the distribution of scale posts in primary schools confirm the continuing association of management with men even in this predominantly female work world.

Marshall (1984) acknowledges the power of the stereotype of appropriate behaviour for women to allow less self determination and less personal rights than stereotypes of masculinity. Like Cunnison, she also shows how those who choose not to break the stereotype (and risk the disapprobation of male peers) still achieve what they want through other means; for example, in the different use of power. Rather than using power agentically (i.e. assuming it to be competitive, controlling, owned by the individual and expressed through doing) she describes women managers' 'communion' approach which uses power co-operatively, based on joint ownership, directed towards influence and expressed in the individual's quality of being.

Women managers' preference for what Marshall calls 'communion' as a guiding principle for managing others in education is reflected in Gray (1987), Jayne (1989), Jones (1990), Powney and Weiner (1991) and Acker (1992). It is a matter of concern that so many of these mainly exploratory and small scale studies are quoted so widely as fact. Gray's proposals about distinctions between masculine and feminine styles are a good example. They are not research based but draw on his experiences of training programmes for education managers. He starts with the hypothesis that primary schools are predominantly feminine organisations and secondary schools masculine. The criteria for making this distinction are not given. The hypothesis is challengeable by those teachers in both sectors who are uncomfortable with the notion that their main purpose is to nurture (primary) or control (secondary). According to Gray, the gender-based association of characteristics creates problems for men at primary level, particularly headteachers who may not have the appropriate nurturing characteristics, and women at secondary level the required controlling abilities. Unusually for a discussion of gender considerations in educational management he mainly addresses the problems for men, particularly in primary school management, in recognising and using the 'female' side of their nature. In his view many heads are ineffective at management because they fear the feminine qualities this calls on (p.302). Presumably he is here assuming headteachers to be men.

Although his discussion begs a whole range of questions about his unproblematic ascription of 'male' and 'female' characteristics to one or other sex, it introduces into the debate about stereotypes of headship behaviour the need to consider the extent to which they operate for both men and women. If, as recent study has shown, (Bolam *et al.*, 1993) effective school leadership relates to leadership styles that are democratic, collegial, open, consultative and team oriented, and these styles are more evident in women's management styles, the implications for selection and management development are considerable. Jayne's argument is similar to Gray's, based on her experiences of working with men and women managers in primary schools. Her starting point is that there are differences in their approaches to management. The differences are not innate (as Gray appears to claim) but the outcome of different socialisation patterns and life experiences. For example, she has observed differences in how new heads brought change into schools; 'men tell, women only use coercion as a last resort' (p.111). She argues that women's different use of power is the outcome of the fact that they have less power in society and are therefore less likely to abuse it when they have it. Her conclusion is that training courses need to pay more attention to 'traditional female qualities' and target not just women but those with whom they work, to eliminate different expectations of men and women as leaders.

Johnston (1986) in a carefully constructed study of gender differences in teachers' preferences for primary school leadership attempted to measure expectations of leadership styles. Using a modification of the Ohio Leadership Behaviour Description Questionnaire (LBDQ) with a group of primary school teachers in Northern Ireland, he found that men and women teachers had different conceptions of their ideal man and woman headteacher. Men wanted men leaders to combine direction and co-ordination; women wanted men leaders to be authoritative and facilitative. Men wanted women leaders to be facilitative and directing; women wanted women leaders to co-ordinate and control. Inevitably his findings are coloured by the androcentrism of the instrument on which his questionnaire is based. The Ohio LBDQ focused on 'head men' in mainstream formal organisations. They point clearly, however, to the role played by the expectations of colleagues and others in shaping leadership behaviour. Johnston concludes that there could be problems if women model their leadership behaviour on men's, though he does not make the same claim for men using women's leadership behaviour as a model. His study, like many others, is also limited by the fact that it looks only at expectations of behaviour rather than how school leaders actually behave. A similar study at secondary school level could provide a useful basis for comparison and extend the debate about the extent to which primary and secondary schools represent respectively 'feminine' and 'masculine' cultures which have repercussions for the conceptualisation of management.

Jones' (1990) study of men and women teachers' attitudes to promotion found some differences in their expectations of themselves and others as leaders. Based on what they said rather than what they did, both men and women favoured a democratic model of management which they saw both men and women heads as capable of providing. However, while men saw themselves as more innovative than women in introducing change, women did not see their male colleagues in this way. Women preferred to use staff expertise in bringing about change, men drew on adviser support and expertise. Interestingly, given Ball's point about men's relatively negative attitudes to the exploration of gender issues, Jones had a 100 per cent response from women teachers in her sample, and only 66 per cent from men, many of whom thought the study sexist (p.12).

Powney and Weiner (1991) describe the strategies used by the women and black managers they interviewed to fight back against the obstacles they faced once in senior positions. The problems included: invisibility (being treated as though they were juniors); visibility (being stereotyped); tokenism (assumed to be there for political reasons only); hostility, harassment, patronage and exploitation. A number commented on their isolation, a sense of people waiting to see them fall. The authors question the implications of this sense of isolation when set against the expressed preference of most for a democratic style of leadership (p.25). They suggest that potential conflict between the two positions (of being isolated and encouraging participation) might explain the group of six white women whose style is described as 'self doubting', that is they advocate one management style but use another. Black women managers in their sample were least likely to use participative approaches to management. The study thus provides a useful basis for considering differences in women's management styles as well as similarities. The descriptions of style are based solely, however, on the interviewee's own comments and are not checked against others' perceptions of how they behave or observation of their practice.

Taken together, the studies described barely begin to scratch the surface of a gender-influenced description of school leadership styles. The limitations are less the fault of the authors, more the absence of adequate funding to explore these issues at length and in depth. Exponents of the debate about differences in style distinguish their positions in terms of the extent to which they are essentialists (women are 'naturally' different from men) or believe that how women behave as managers is determined by how they are seen and treated, as well as their personal characteristics. It was suggested earlier that the debate needs to be set in the context of the concept of 'androgynous manager' a term which derives from the work of Sandra Bem (1977). As a psychological term androgyny suggests that it is possible for people to exhibit both masculine and feminine qualities and that such qualities are present in both men and women. Sex role stereotyping has tended to polarise the qualities, so that 'masculine' characteristics are associated only with men and feminine with women. At their extremes both sets of characteristics become negative. Advocates of androgynous approaches to management argue for an integration of the characteristics so that management behaviours incorporate both masculine and feminine behaviours. According to this model managers in schools, whether men or women, would be able to draw on both male and female qualities as the situation required. If empirical research based on observation was able to show that this is what effective leaders do, then contingency theories of leadership would need to be modified to take account of the new data. At the moment, the assumption is that effective leaders use contingency styles (Hoyle 1986) drawing from their repertoire of management skills and knowledge to fit the situation. What the theory has not so far addressed is whether men and women draw on different repertoires or repertoires that are limited by perceptions of gender-appropriate behaviour.

Conclusions

There is relatively little to date in research about women managers in education that can be used to challenge theories of educational management or lead to their reconceptualisation to include both women and men. Although definitions of career that do not work for women have been questioned, there is still only a limited quantitative research base in Britain about the career routes of both men and women teachers. The picture is even more sparse in further and higher education. Research by Hall *et al.* (1986) and Weindling and Earley (1987) provided portraits mainly of men administrators in education. The NDC's current research on women headteachers will seek to redress the balance by examining a solely female view of the school world and by providing some of the missing biographies of women administrators so that more is known of the individual lives of women who occupy these positions.

Other research is needed that challenges traditional stereotypes of what constitutes appropriate management behaviour and process. The association of management and masculinity has not been established as a fact yet it is treated as such, with negative consequences for women in education. Observation studies of managers at work in non-educational settings (Mintzberg 1973, Stewart 1982) make no distinction between men and women in the job and are based primarily on men. Hypotheses about women's style of management and its congruence with effective education management strategies, if proven, may well lead to a reversal of Professor Higgins plea, so that selectors and developers in education will cry 'why can't a man be more like a woman'. Then both theory and prescriptions for action will truly have been transformed by the inclusion of gender as a relevant concept for understanding educational management.

References

Acker, S. (1980) 'Women: the other academics' *British Journal of the Sociology of Education* **1**, 1, 81–91.

Acker, S. (1992) 'Gender, collegiality and teachers' workplace culture in Britain: in search of the women's culture', paper presented at AERA, San Francisco, April.

Acker, S. (ed.) (1989) *Teachers, Gender and Careers* Lewes: The Falmer Press.

Alexander, R.J., Willcocks, J. and Kinder, K. (1989) *Changing Primary Practice* London: The Falmer Press.

Al-Khalifa, E. (1989).

Al-Khalifa, E. and Migniuolo, F. (1990) 'Messages for Management: the Experiences of Women's Training', paper given at the Conference on Equal Advances in Education Management, Vienna 3–6 December 1990.

AMMA (1985) *Women Teachers' Career Prospects — 1985: An AMMA Research Study* London: AMMA.

AUT (Scotland) (1989) *The Situation of Women Members in Scottish Universities: a questionnaire study* Edinburgh: Association of University Teachers.

Ball, S. (1987) *The Micropolitics of the School* London: Methuen.

Bem, S. (1977) *Psychological Androgyny* West Publishing Company.

Bolam, R., McMahon, A., Pocklington, K. and Weindling, D. (1993) *Effective Management in Schools* London: HMSO

Byrne Whyte, J. (1987) 'Under-representation of women in management posts in education: a critique of two theoretical explanatory accounts' in Unterkircher, L. and Wagner, I. (eds) *Die Andre halfte der Gesellschaft Verlag des Osterreichischen Gewerkschaftsbunden.*

Cunnison, S. (1985) 'Making it in a Man's World: Women Teachers in a Senior High School', Occasional Paper No. 1, University of Hull.

David, M. (1989) 'Prima Donna inter Pares? Women in Academic Management' in Acker, S. (ed.) (1989) *op. cit.*

Davidson, H. (1985) 'Unfriendly Myths about Women Teachers' in Whyte, J. *et al.* (eds) *Girl Friendly Schooling* London: Methuen.

Earley, P. and Weindling, D. (1988) 'Heading for the top: The career paths of secondary school heads' *Educational Management and Administration* **16**, 1.

Evetts, J. (1986) 'Teachers' careers: the objective dimension *Educational Studies* **12**, 3, 225–244.

Evetts, J. (1987) 'Becoming career ambitious: the career strategies of married women who became primary headteachers in the 1960s and 1970s' *Educational Review* **39**, 1, 15–29.
Evetts, J. (1990) *Women in Primary Teaching: Career Contexts and Strategies* London: Unwin Hyman.
Evetts, J. (1991) 'The experience of secondary headship selection: continuity and change' *Educational Studies* **17**, 3, 285–294.
Fullan, M. (1991) *The New Meaning of Educational Change* London: Cassell.
Grant, R. (1989) 'Women teachers' career pathways: Towards an alternative model of career' in Acker, S. (ed.) (1989) *op. cit.*
Gray, H.L. (1987) 'Gender considerations in school management' *School Organisation* **17**, 3, 297–302.
Hall, V., Mackay, H. and Morgan, C. (1986) *Headteachers at Work* Milton Keynes: Open University Press
Hilsum, S. and Start, K.B. (1974) *Promotion and Careers in Teaching* Slough: NFER.
Hough, J. (1986) 'Gender bias in educational management and administration' *Educational Management and Administration* **16**, 69–74.
Hunter, J. (1987) *Women's Careers in Secondary and Primary Teaching: the Birmingham Study* London: ILEA.
Inner London Education Authority (1984) *Womens' Careers in Teaching: a Survey of Teachers' Views* London: ILEA.
Jayne, E. (1989) 'Women as leaders of schools: the role of training' *Educational Management and Administration* **17**, 3, 109–114.
Jenkins, H.O. (1991) *Getting it Right: A Handbook for Successful School Leadership* Oxford: Blackwell.
Johnston, J. (1986) 'Gender differences in teachers' preferences for primary school leadership,' *Educational Management and Administration* **14**, 219–226.
Jones, A. (1987) *Leadership for Tomorrow's Schools* Oxford: Basil Blackwell Ltd.
Jones, K. (1990) 'The attitudes of men and women primary school teachers to promotion' *Educational Management and Administration* **18**, 3, July.
Kanter, R.M. (1977) *Men and Women of the Corporation* New York: Basic Books.
Lyon, K. and West, J. (1992) 'The trouble with equal opportunities: The case of women academics', paper presented to the Conference on Social Order in Post Classical Sociology, to mark the retirement of Professor Michael Banton, 8–10 September, University of Bristol.
Marshall, J. (1984) *Women Managers: Travellers in a Male World* Chichester: John Wiley and Sons.
Martini, R. *et al.* (1984) *Women's Careers in Teaching: Survey of Teachers' Views* London: ILEA.
McBurney, E. and Hough, J. (1989) 'Role perceptions of female deputy heads' *Educational Management and Administration* **17**, 115–118.
Mintzberg, H. (1973) *The Nature of Managerial Work* New York: Harper and Row.
Morgan, C., Hall, V. and Mackay, H. (1983) *The Selection of Secondary Headteachers* Milton Keynes: Open University Press.

Mortimore, P. and Mortimore, J. (eds) (1991) *The Secondary Head: Roles, Responsibilities and Reflections* London: Paul Chapman.
National Union of Teachers (1980) *Promotion and the Woman Teachers* London: NUT.
Nias, J. (1989) *Primary Teachers Talking: a Study of Teaching as Work* London: Routledge.
Ozga, J. (ed.) (1992) *Women in Educational Management* Buckingham: Open University Press.
Powney, J. and Weiner, G. (1991) *Outside of the Norm: Equity and Management in Educational Institutions* South Bank Polytechnic: Department of Education.
Riches, C. (1989) 'Gender and School Management' in Saran, R. and Trafford, V. (eds) *Research in Education Management and Policy* Lewes: Falmer Press.
Sargent, A. (1983) *The Androgynous Manager: Blending Male and Female Management Styles for Today's Organization* New York: American Management Association.
Schmuck, P. (1986) 'School management and administration: an analysis by gender' in Hoyle, E. and McMahon, A. (eds) *World Yearbook: The Management of Schools* London: Kogan Page.
Schmuck, P. (1987) 'Gender: A relevant concept for educational leadership', paper prepared for the National Graduate Research Seminar in Educational Administration, University Council for Educational Administration, 24 April, Washington DC.
Shakeshaft, C. (1989) (2nd edn) *Women in Educational Administration* Newbury Park, California: Sage Publications.
Shakeshaft, C. (1989) (updated edition) *Women in Educational Administration* Newbury Park, California: Sorwin Press Inc.
Sikes, P., Measor, L. and Woods, P. (1985) *Teacher Careers: Crises and Continuities* Lewes: Falmer Press.
Spencer, A., Finlayson, N. and Crabb, S. (1987) 'Women in further and higher education' *Coombe Lodge Report* **20**, 3: FESC.
Stewart, R. (1982) *Choices for the Manager: a Guide to Managerial Work and Behaviour* Maidenhead: McGraw-Hill.
Torrington, D. and Weightman, J. (1987) *The Reality of School Management* Oxford: Blackwell
Trown, E. and Needham, G. (1980) *Reduction in Part-time Teaching: Implications for Schools and Women Teachers* Manchester: Equal Opportunities Commission
Turner, G. and Clift, P. (1988) *Studies in Teacher Appraisal* London: Falmer Press.
Wallace, M. and Hall, V. (1993) *Senior Management Teams in Action* London: Paul Chapman (in the press).
Weightman, J. (1989) 'Women in management' *Educational Management and Administration* **17**, 3, Summer.
Weindling, D. and Earley, P. (1987) *Secondary Headship: The First Years* Slough: NFER-Nelson.
Williams, H. (1981) 'The role of the deputy head. Is it changing? A study with particular reference to women in management in large comprehensive schools during the last five years' *CORE* **5**, 1, March.

4 Women in educational management in the United States

Charol Shakeshaft

While women are the majority of teachers in most of the classrooms in the United States, they do not hold the majority of the positions of formal leadership. Current studies of gender balance in school administration indicate that the majority of school administrators are still men (Saks 1992). This chapter will document the under-representation of women in school administration, report the data on female administrative effectiveness, review the research which identifies the barriers to women who aspire to school leadership in primary and secondary schools, and give examples of where work on gender and leadership in schools is moving in the United States.

An examination of the research on women school administrators in different settings reveals that the first thing researchers want to know is how many and at what levels are women represented in school administration. Once women's under-representation has been documented, researchers pursue data that help to explain why women do not hold more positions in school management. A subset of this strand of work compares male and female administrators in an effort to answer the question, 'Are women not hired because they aren't as good as men?' This focus often leads to the study of female styles of leadership, irrespective of male norms. Finally, work is being done to examine gender issues in communication styles and leadership in school administration.

Representation of women in school administration

Trying to document the number of women in school administration in the US is difficult: administrative titles and jobs are not comparable across districts and the US Department of Education does not record administrative positions by sex for the over 14,000 school districts in the United States. However, as nearly as we can tell, 10.5 per cent of school superintendents, 12 per cent of secondary principals and 34 per cent of elementary principals are women (Jones and Montenegro 1990, Saks 1992).

Female performance as school managers

Numerous studies have been published which document how well women perform in administrative positions in schools. In a synthesis of hundreds of studies comparing the administrative styles and effectiveness of male and female school managers, women were found to do as well or better than men on the variables studied (Shakeshaft 1987). This synthesis, as well as other reviews of work from the United States, indicates the following gender differences for males and females (Driver 1990, Ortiz and Marshall 1988, Shakeshaft 1987).

Relationships

Women spend more time with people, communicate more, care more about individual differences, are concerned more with teachers and marginal students, and motivate more than do men. Not suprisingly, staffs of women administrators rate women higher, are more productive, and have higher morale than staffs of male administrators. Students in schools with women principals also have higher morale and are more involved in student affairs. Further, parents are more favorable toward schools and districts run by women and thus more involved in school life than are parents in schools run by men.

Teaching and learning

Women administrators are more instrumental in instructional learning than men and they exhibit greater knowledge of teaching methods and techniques. Women administrators are not only more likely than men to emphasise achievement, they are also more likely to co-ordinate instructional programmes and evaluate student progress. In these schools and districts, women administrators know their teachers and they know the academic progress of their students. Women are more likely than men to help new teachers and to supervise all teachers directly. Women also create a school climate more conducive to learning, one that is more orderly, safer, and quieter. Not suprisingly, academic achievement is higher in schools and districts in which women are administrators than in those run by men.

Community

Building community is an essential part of a woman administrator's style. From speech patterns to decision-making styles, women exhibit a more democratic, participatory style that encourages inclusiveness rather than exclusiveness. Women involve themselves more with staff and students, ask for and get higher participation, and maintain more closely knit organisations than do men. Staffs of women principals have higher job satisfaction and are more engaged in their work than those of male administrators. These staffs are also more aware of and committed to the goals of learning and the members of the staffs have more shared professional goals. These are schools and districts in which teachers receive a great deal of support from their female administrators. They are also districts and schools where achievement is emphasised.

Barriers to women aspiring to be school administrators

If women are as good or better than men, why aren't there more of them as school administrators? Studies that examine the barriers that keep women from becoming school administrators document a number of reasons which have prevented women from moving into formal leadership positions in schools.

Devaluation of women

The factor that explains the most about the resistance to women in positions of power in schools is the devaluation of women. Women are seen as less than and different from men (Bernard 1981). This assignment of less value to women takes the form of attitudes that favour males over females for administrative positions. Literally hundreds of studies indicate that negative attitudes toward women by those who hire constitute the major barrier to female advancement in school administration (Shakeshaft 1987).

These negative attitudes become discriminatory actions when women seek administrative positions. Particular discriminatory practices that have been documented include the following filters (Timpano and Knight 1976):

- word of mouth recruiting with only males;
- not allowing outside candidates to apply;
- asking biased interview questions of women, particularly questions about family responsibilities;
- offering women lower salaries than men and refusing to negotiate salaries with women;
- separating applications by sex and interviewing men by quota and not qualifications;

- using criteria not related to performance — such as requiring a certain number of years in a particular position — which screens women out;
- allowing men to skip steps on the career ladder but requiring women to have completed all steps;
- counting as leadership experience typically male activities such as the military but not counting typical female activities such as work in volunteer organisations or the familly;
- interviewing men who don't have the minimum educational and job requirements, but requiring women to hold all the qualifications before they can be considered for an interview;
- having only men as interviewers;
- asking women how their husbands feel about them becoming a school administrator.

Most of the reason why women do not become school administrators can be explained by understanding that women are not valued as much as men and that this bias results in negative attitudes and practices toward women aspiring to be school administrators.

Many of these practices are subtle and are not coded by either the receiver or the giver as biased. For instance, studies of women in school administration which ask them if they have ever been discriminated against, often find that the majority of women say no. And yet, if these same women are given a list of discriminatory actions and asked if these things have ever happened to them, the majority will say yes. The pressure to internalise societal bias as well as the lack of understanding about what sex discrimination looks like, means that even women don't recognise what has happened to them. Nevertheless, the overwhelming evidence identifies sex discrimination as the number one barrier to women in school administration (Al-Khalifa and Migniulo 1990, Driver 1990, Gerver and Hart 1990, Nylen and Sorhuus 1990, Shakeshaft 1987).

Support systems/family responsibilities

A second explanation of why women do not become school administrators is that they lack the support systems to help them find and secure jobs. Women are much less likely than men to have formal or informal networks that let them know about jobs and help them get interviewed. Further, in most families, women are still responsible for the majority of childcare and homemaking. Although there is no documentation that such responsibilities inhibit the ability of women to perform their jobs, there is a belief by many who hire that such responsibilities make women undesirable candidates for administrative positions.

At the same time, women sometimes say that family responsibilities keep them from applying for and assuming administrative positions not because these women don't think they could do everything, but because they believe the costs would be too high for their families and themselves.

Self esteem/self confidence

Studies indicate that females have lower self confidence than do males (AAUW 1991). This lowered confidence level helps to explain why males are more likely to apply for jobs for which they are both qualified and not qualified and why females generally only apply for jobs for which they are highly qualified. Females rarely apply for positions for which they are not qualified. As a result, there are usually more male applications for a position and a male — even a less qualified male — is likely to be hired.

Lack of self esteem also helps to explain why females internalise failure and males externalise it. Thus, when a male doesn't get a job, he most likely blames an outside factor. Females, on the other hand, are much more likely to believe that the reason they weren't hired was because they weren't good enough. Since studies indicate that it takes females four times as many interviews to land their first position as males, it is not surprising that many females quit looking (Shakeshaft 1987). Instead of considering that one possible and probable reason for their rejection is sex bias, females are more likely to code their rejection as personal failure and decide that they weren't cut out for school administration in the first place.

Aspiration level

The folklore about the lack of women in school administration tells us that women aren't in formal positions of leadership because they don't want to be. Studies of female aspiration level don't support this myth and indicate that if women believe that it is possible for them to be hired as school administrators, they are likely to aspire to these positions (Kanter 1977, Wheatley 1981). It is only when women believe that becoming a school administrator is impossible that they say they have no interest in such positions.

There are women who have indicated that the tasks of administration are not of interest to them because they entered education to teach. However, as these women come to understand that administration takes many forms, they are also likely to show more interest in becoming administrators. Likewise, studies of women administrators indicate that they do the job differently than do men, focusing more on teaching, learning, and children (Shakeshaft 1987). The more women see other women administrators incorporating the values of teaching, learning, and contact with children, the more likely women are to decide they are interested in becoming school administrators.

Preparation

Studies of the formal preparation needed to become school administrators indicate that in countries where there are certification or educational requirements, women are just as likely as men to have these qualifications.

Visibility

Men tend to be more visible in school life than are women. They are more likely to coach sports and to lead the marching band or orchestra. Additionally, studies indicate that women are less likely to be given the opportunity to take on informal leadership positions within the school than are men. Men are more likely to be asked to chair committees or to represent the school than are women. This visibility gives men an edge over women when it comes to hiring, since these men will already have been seen in leadership positions. To further complicate matters, women have been taught that a womanly virtue is modesty; thus, women are more likely to give others credit for the work they have done.

Gender differences in leadership

To undertand gender differences, it is important to make some distinctions between sex and gender. Sex is a biological description, one that divides most of humankind into two types of people — females and males. Gender is a cultural term. It is socially constructed and describes the characteristics that we ascribe to people because of their sex, the ways we believe they behave or the characteristics we believe they have based upon our cultural expectations of what is male and what is female. As far as I can determine from my work and the work of others, one's biological identification as male or female has very little to do with how people behave and the work they do in schools. However, one's gender identification has a tremendous influence on behaviour, perceptions and effectiveness.

Interestingly, gender has somehow become identified, and in some cases become synonymous, with women. That's unfortunate, since it has led to some confusion both about the direction and the importance of research that examines the influence of gender on organisational dynamics. Research on men is still seen as mainstream and central, while research on women and/or gender issues (both male and female) is often considered a special topic and not central to the understanding of organisational behaviour. It is not surprising, then, that research in educational administration is weak both in research on women in organisations and research on the impact of gender on behaviour. Traditional research for theory and practice has neglected both the female experience and the influence of gender on actions and outcomes; it is both androcentric and gender barren (Shakeshaft and Hanson 1986).

Analysis of the foundation that dominates the fields of educational administration and organisational behaviour indicates that these theories are based upon a white male behaviour and world view. For instance, examination of some of the most cited theories in educational administration and management texts — social systems models, two factor leadership behaviour models, organisational climate research, situational leadership research, and motivational research — indicates that these theories are not only based upon studies of white men, they don't hold up when applied to women and people of colour (Shakeshaft 1987, Shakeshaft and Nowell 1984).

The following sections will explore some of the areas in studies showing that the behaviour of women differs from that of men and the gender interactions that must be considered if we are to build a knowledge base that explains more of human behaviour in organisations than what we can currently account for. While the research discussed in these sections was conducted in schools, the work of others in private sector enterprises indicate that the findings would be similar in those settings (Ferguson 1984).

Gender as an explanatory variable in theories and practice in supervision

Although the area of supervision abounds with theories and scripts, little has been written on the impact of gender on successful supervision. This issue seems particularly salient given the sex structuring of schools which results in an organisation in which males most often supervise females. It takes on added importance if we examine the sex stereotypic expectations of behaviour and status and imagine what implications they might have when the norm is reversed and a female supervises a male.

Thus, gender and gender expectations may partially determine how supervisors interact with those they supervise. For instance, research tells us that the sex of participants affects what is communicated and how it is communicated (Borisoff and Merrill 1985). The same words spoken by a male supervisor have different meanings to male and female teachers. Conversely, an interaction between a female principal and a male teacher is not the same as an exchange between a female principal and a female teacher.

We know that men and women communicate differently and that they listen for different information (Borisoff and Merrill 1985; Tannen 1990). It may be that in a supervisory conference in which a principal is discussing an instructional issue with the teacher, the woman participant is listening for the feeling and the man for the facts. It may also be, given what we know of the values that males and females carry into their jobs in schools, that the woman is focused upon an instructional issue or a matter concerning the child, while the man has chosen to discuss an administrative problem.

Further, research tells us that there may be discomfort in communicating with a member of the other sex. Certainly, we know that male teachers exhibit more hostility in dealing with female administrators than do female teachers. We also know that women administrators have to work harder to get male teachers to 'hear' them (Lee, in press).

Perceptions of competence may also influence supervisory styles and effectiveness. We know that women are initially evaluated less favourably than equally competent men (Shakeshaft 1987), and that males evaluate females more harshly than females evaluate females (Lee, in press). These perceptions may unknowingly affect supervisory interactions, both when the woman is being supervised and when she is the supervisor.

Nowhere does the impact of gender on supervision become more evident than in the area of feedback. Men receive both more and a wider range of feedback than do women. Women are more likely to get non-evaluative feedback, or neutral responses. Men receive both more positive and more negative responses.

Shakeshaft (1987) found that male administrators are less likely to give direct feedback to females but more likely to give it to males. For instance, when a male subordinate makes a mistake or doesn't live up to the expectations of his boss, his supervisor tends to level with him, 'telling it like it is'. When a female errs, she often isn't even informed. Instead, the mistake is corrected by others without her knowledge. The results are two-fold. For the male, learning takes place instantly. He gets criticism and the chance to change his behaviour. He learns to deal with negative opinions of his work and has the option of improving.

Females often never hear anything negative, being given neutral or slightly positive cues even if their performance is less than ideal. This results in a woman's misconception of her abilities or at least the level of her performance. If she isn't directly told that her work is not meeting expectations she has neither the opportunity to improve nor the opportunity to reassess her abilities.

These differential feedback patterns are not unique to the adult work setting. The work of Sadker and Sadker (1986) describes similar patterns throughout K–12 schooling, where boys receive more feedback and a wider range of feedback. These early differences not only help us to understand why we behave as we do when we become adult workers, they also help us to understand women's reactions to criticism in the rare instances when they get it first-hand (women always get criticism, the issue is whether or not they get to hear it).

In interviews with women administrators (Shakeshaft 1987) the women were found to take criticism hard. They tend to think it is an assessment of their very essence. The first time they receive criticism or the first time they fail, women administrators code it as a sign that they are inferior and that they never should have tried to become an administrator in the first place. This is hardly surprising for two reasons. First, females in this society are less valued than men. Because of this, women, from birth onward through school and into adult life, receive subtle and not so subtle messages about their worth. These messages are one of the reasons that women have been found to have lower self images and less self esteem than men. Secondly, if, as girls, females received very little direct criticism, women have hardly been given the opportunities to learn not to take critical comments personally. This lack of experience lends itself to an understanding of why supervisors of women tend to shy away from giving them this critical feedback.

In interviews with male superintendents and principals asking them why they didn't confront women with their misgivings and dissatisfactions, one of the major reasons that was given was the fear of hurting women's feelings and making them cry (Shakeshaft 1987). Most of the men were uncomfortable with the prospect of tears. When questioned about what they expected from men to whom they gave negative feedback, most anticipated anger. While none of the administrators in this study liked confronting anyone with negative feedback, the prospect of an angry response was easier to face than the prospect of tears. Male superintendents and principals said they didn't like to deal with angry subordinates, but that they had the skills to do so. They were much less comfortable with crying, and because of this discomfort most failed to give women important corrective feedback that would have allowed the women to improve their performance as educators. This fear of tears led us to examine who cries and how often. What we found was that there is not a lot of crying in public schools, and that although women cry in front of supervisors slightly more than men, the difference in frequency is very small. However, women are reported to cry equally often in front of females and males while males only cried in front of women. Thus, we learn that it is the fear of tears — rather than overwhelming evidence of actual crying — that paralyses male administrators. We also learn that both men and women cry, so it isn't solely a 'female' problem. Finally, we learn to understand that although it is not solely a female problem, and although nobody cries very much, the fear of tears or the gender expectations about what women do, keep women from getting honest feedback about their performance and impairs the effectiveness of the supervisory styles of male administrators.

The importance of this discussion about supervisory styles and feedback is that gender perceptions are influencing behaviour and interfering with effectiveness. Because of our beliefs about who men are and who women are, many administrative actions are censored or changed depending upon who we are interacting with. The issues are difficult for both men and women. Women must be aware of the feedback loop and try to determine if they are getting helpful evaluative information. Men, on the other hand, often perceive themselves in a 'damned if you do, damned if you don't' position. If a man treats a woman as he does a man, he may be accused of being harsh or unfair. If he doesn't treat a woman in the same manner, he may be accused of not giving her helpful or corrective feedback. We need to examine our expectations about male and female behaviour and confront the issue so that both men and women are as effective as they can be in a supervisory relationship.

The studies of behaviour led to an examination of whether or not the written evaluations of job performance are different when done by males and females. Specifically, an investigation of whether or not there were differences in the written evaluations of teachers by male and female principals was undertaken, using my earlier work (1987) as a guide for exploring this issue.

In this study (Shakeshaft, Nowell and Perry 1991), a content analysis was done of the written evaluations of 108 female teachers by eight principals (five males and three females) to determine whether or not male and female principals highlighted different things. All of the principals worked in the same school district and all had received the same amount of training in the Hunter technique. The evaluations were coded without knowledge of the sex of the principal; inter-rater reliability was 77 per cent.

We did find some differences in the things that women and men focused on. Women were more likely than men to encourage the empowerment of their teachers, to establish instructional priorities, to be attentive to the social and emotional development of the students, to focus on student relationships, to be attentive to the feelings of teachers, to include more 'facts' in the evaluation, to look for the teacher's personal effects on the lives of children, to place emphasis on the technical skills of teaching, to make comments on the content and quality of the educational programme to provide information gathered from other sources, to involve the teacher in decision-making, to issue directives for improvement, to provide immediate feedback on performance, and to emphasise curricular programmes. Men, on the other hand, were more likely than women to emphasise organisational structure and to avoid conflict.

These findings support the literature that women may approach the supervisory process by valuing different characteristics, and thus concentrating on a different set of criteria, than do men. This study suggests that even when trained in a similar approach to supervisory interaction, males and females may still bring with them expectations and behaviours based upon gender. While this study is in no way definitive, it does provide us with some additional support for why we need to understand more fully gender in all aspects of school administration, especially supervision.

Sexuality and administrative behaviour

While administrators often joke about sex, they seldom examine how their attitudes and beliefs about their own sexuality guide their administrative behaviour. While both males and females are uncomfortable with sexual issues, male discomfort serves as a larger impediment to effective administration than does female discomfort for three reasons: (i) there are more male administrators at every level in schools than there are female administrators; (ii) females have had to learn to understand a white male world to succeed in it, and therefore, are more likely to have already dealt with issues of sexuality; and (iii) women and men have been socialised differently around the issues of sexuality, and female socialisation is less likely to be the kind that impairs effective administrative functioning than is male socialisation.

Sexual issues shape many management strategies. For instance, hiring practices, organisational climate and team building are all affected by fears, discomfort or displays of sexuality. The following briefly examines how sexuality — and in particular heterosexuality — interacts with some typical management behaviours and, more specifically, how male discomfort with the sexual self impedes effective management. Throughout the analysis of the role sexuality plays in management issues is the issue of gender. Without rigid gender roles, sexuality issues would not be so potent. It is because of the gender expectation of a woman's sexual purpose that sexuality becomes an issue.

An example of how beliefs about sexuality affect administrative behaviour can be found in an examination of who male administrators hire and why. In a study of the hiring practices of male superintendents (Shakeshaft 1989) we asked these superintendents if they would hire an attractive female. Almost all of the superintendents in our study said, 'Sure, I'd hire an attractive woman.' When we asked for what job, almost all had her slotted for an elementary principalship. When we followed up and asked if these superintendents would hire this imaginary woman as an assistant superintendent, in a role that worked very closely with the superintendent, very few of the superintendents said they would. The issue for them was the combination of the intensity of the working relationship and the attractiveness of the woman. Most admitted that they felt uncomfortable in a close working relationship with an attractive woman.

Some, however, not only did not feel uncomfortable, but said they had, indeed, hired a woman to work closely with them, usually as assistant superintendent. Therefore, we interviewed both groups of superintendents about their beliefs or experiences with hiring women in an attempt to get an understanding of some of the issues that might surface when men think about working closely with women.

The first reason superintendents gave for not hiring a woman to work closely with them was their concern that school board members would see something unseemly in the relationship and that this perception would threaten the superintendent's effectiveness with their boards. We interviewed those superintendents who had hired a woman and asked them if they had received negative feedback from board members. While a few reported suggestive comments or sexual jokes from board members, they all said that they in no way felt that working with a woman had hurt their reputations or threatened their effectiveness in the eyes of the board.

The second reason the superintendents gave for not hiring attractive women was their worry that it would cause marital friction and few wanted the additional stress of 'trouble on the homefront' added to their already stressful lives. Interviews with those superintendents who had hired women indicated they didn't find this a problem. None of these superintendents reported the jealousy or friction that their colleagues anticipated. However, the fear of jealousy wasn't confined to superintendents who didn't hire women. The women assistant superintendents worried about the possibility and reported that they made a special effort to build a relationship with the wife of their 'boss'. In an attempt to 'avoid problems', these women assistant superintendents described ways in which they tried to ensure that the wives of the men to whom they reported would not worry about romantic relationships between their husbands and themselves.

The third reason that the superintendents gave for not hiring a woman with whom to work closely is that most of the male superintendents said they wouldn't feel comfortable working closely with an attractive woman because these men weren't sure they wouldn't be sexually attracted to her. And if they were, it seemed to them like a no-win situation. If the superintendent were attracted to his female subordinate and she didn't return the feelings, the superintendent felt he ran the risk of being charged with sexual harrassment. On the other hand, if she were similarly attracted, the superintendent's first two fears (school board disapproval and marital discord) might become reality. Thus, fear of their own lack of sexual control led these superintendents to a position that it was better not to work closely with women. The superintendents who had hired women didn't deny that they might become sexually attracted to the women who worked with them, but what set them apart from their colleagues who would not hire a woman was that these superintendents didn't believe that feeling attracted to a woman meant they had to act on it. In other words, they didn't equate attraction with action.

Thus, in this study, most male superintendents did not want to work closely with women because they saw women as a threat. Because of the superintendents' gender expectations that women are for sex and that women, thus, constitute a sexual danger to the superintendents, most men in our study said they would not hire a woman. This example demonstrates how male discomfort with sexuality and male socialisation of what it is to be a man, keep women from positions in school administration.

Gender and the determination of appropriate and ethical administrative behaviour

Studies of what males and females believe is appropriate and ethical behaviour indicate that both may be coded differently by males and females. In other words, what women think is ethical and appropriate administrative behaviour may not be what men think is ethical and appropriate. An example which illustrates these differences can be found in studies which attempted to determine whether or not men and women superintendents conceptualise their administrative teams differently and whether or not these superintendents and their team members value different traits in team members (Garfinkel 1988, Shakeshaft 1989). Garfinkel found that both men and women value competence and trust, but that they give each a different priority. For women superintendents, competence is the first thing they look for in a team member; trust is lower on the list. Men superintendents, on the other hand, identify trust as their number one criteria for team membership, and view competence as less important. To complicate matters, especially for team members, men and women define trust differently. Men, both superintendents and team members, are more likely to describe trust as the 'ability and comfort to say what they wished to say, confident that the persons they were sharing their thoughts or opinions with would not ridicule or repeat these thoughts elsewhere' (Garfinkel 1988, p.311). Women superintendents defined trust as 'an expectancy held by an individual, that the word, promise or written statement of another individual or group can be relied on' (p.311).

These differing conceptions of trust call for different indicators of proof and illustrate some basic differences men and women give to talk (Shakeshaft, unpublished data). For men to see a person as trustworthy, that person must not divulge information or discuss actions or conversations with others. Men said they assumed that if they told a subordinate something that the subordinate would not tell others unless he or she had been instructed to tell. Men were very clear that a trustworthy subordinate wouldn't talk and that this was such an accepted code of behaviour that the men I interviewed didn't think it necessary to remind subordinates 'not to tell'.

Women saw things very differently. Not only did women not code 'telling something' as disloyal, they said they expected subordinates to tell unless specifically instructed otherwise. They expected people to discuss conversations, actions, and feelings with others. Women went even farther; they said it would be 'wrong' of them to expect people not to discuss issues within their work lives. These women administrators said that talk was important and for them to restrict talk, without an extraordinarily compelling reason, would be inappropriate and unfair.

Here we see two very different expectations. Men believed that subordinates should not and would not discuss issues unless so instructed and that to do so was not only a disloyal act, but the mark of an inexperienced and inept administrator. Women believed that subordinates would talk and had the right to talk about issues they had discussed, and the women superordinates believed that to instruct subordinates otherwise was wrong and immoral.

Women did code some behaviour as untrustworthy. What women saw as untrustworthy was someone failing to do what they said they would do, when they said they would do it. Men didn't identify a person as untrustworthy if he or she didn't deliver on time. Rather, they saw that as a time management or competency issue.

Thus, women supervisors would talk about a person's lack of loyalty or that they couldn't trust that person if he or she hadn't done the work. Men described a subordinate as untrustworthy if he or she discussed issues with others without permission.

In addition to these differing perceptions of trust and loyalty by superordinates, these studies found that subordinates also held polar views of how a loyal team member should act. Men team members, for instance, said that the way they would show loyalty was to not disagree with the 'boss', except in a private conversation. Even if they didn't think the boss was right, men team members said that to be loyal they would need to support whatever the boss did. These male team members said that if they couldn't go along with the boss's agenda without major disagreement, the only honorable thing for them to do would be to find another job. Female team members conceptualised loyal and ethical behaviour differently. Over and over they said that a loyal team member was one who spoke up when he or she disagreed with the course of action the boss was taking. These women would say, 'It is my responsibility as a professional to let my boss know when I disagree. It would be unethical and unprofessional of me to keep quiet if I didn't think my boss's idea was a good one. It would be immoral not to speak up'. These two conceptualisations by team members were carried through in the ways the male and female superintendents coded loyal and ethical behaviour. Thus, male superintendents described subordinates as disloyal for publically disagreeing, while female superintendents coded subordinates as disloyal for not speaking up.

The point of examining these differences is not to say one approach is right and one is wrong (the way theory and practice up to now have done), but rather to help us understand that males and females may be coming from very different places, and that unless we understand these differences, we aren't likely to work well together.

Conclusions

Women are under-represented in school administration in US elementary and secondary schools. Although women perform as good or better as school administrators than men, they are less likely to be hired as school managers. While there are a number of barriers that women can address, the major barrier to women in school administration is sex discrimination, an obstacle that can only be effectively confronted at a societal level. Finally, gender interacts in two ways in studying leadership. In the first instance, women and men may approach administration differently based upon their socialisation patterns as females and males. Secondly, gender stereotypes may interfere in the ways women and men work together and, therefore, cause misunderstandings or result in less effective management. Understanding how gender interacts in the management of schools will help us improve that management as well as providing equal access for both females and males to administrative positions.

References

AAUW (1991) *Shortchanging Girls, Shortchanging America* Washington: AAUW.

Al-Khalifa, E. and Migniuolo, F.W. (1990) United Kingdom: Messages for management, the experience of women's training. Paper presented at the Equal Advances in Education Management Conference, Council of Europe, Vienna, Austria.

Bernard, J. (1981) *The Female World* New York: Free Press.

Borisoff, D. and Merrill, L. (1985) *The Power to Communicate: Gender Differences as Barriers* Prospect Heights, Ill: Waveland Press.

Driver, K. (1990) United Kingdom: Quality matters, an initiative in developing school leadership from the secondary heads association paper presented at the Equal Advances in Education Management Conference, Council of Europe, Vienna, Austria.

Ferguson, K.E. (1984) *The Feminist Case against Bureaucracy* Philadelphia: Temple University Press.

Garfinkel, E. (1988) Ways men and women in school administration conceptualize the administrative team. Unpublished doctoral dissertation, Hofstra University, Hempstead, New York.

Gerver, E. and Hart, L. (1990) Surviving in a cold climate: Women and decisionmaking in Scottish education. Paper presented at the Equal Advances in Education Management Conference, Council of Europe, Vienna, Austria.

Jones, E. H. and Montenegro, X. P. (1990) *Women and Minorities in School Administration: Facts and Figures, 1989–1990.* Washington, D. C.: American Association of School Administrators, Office of Minority Affairs.

Kanter, R. M. (1977) *Men and Women of the Corporation* New York: Basic Books.

Lee, V. (in press) *Teachers and Principals: Gender-related Perceptions of Leadership and Power in Secondary Schools.*

Nylen, C. and Sorhuus, E. (1990) Sweden: In search of equality paper presented at the Equal Advances in Education Management Conference, Council of Europe, Vienna, Austria.

Ortiz, F. I. and Marshall, C. (1988) 'Women in educational administration' in *Handbook of Research on Educational Administration* Boyan, N. (ed.) New York: Longman.

Sadker, M. and Sadker, D. (1986) 'Sexism in the classroom: From grade school to graduate school' *Phi Delta Kappan* March, 512–515.

Saks, J. B. (1992) 'Education vital signs' *American School Board Journal* **179**(12), 38.

Shakeshaft, C. (1987) *Women in Educational Administration* Newbury Park: Sage Press. (1989, Corwyn Press.)

Shakeshaft, C. (1989) 'The gender gap in research in educational administration' *Educational Administration Quarterly* **25**(3).

Shakeshaft, C. and Hanson, M. (1986) 'Androcentric bias in the *Educational Administration Quarterly*' *Educational Administration Quarterly* **XXII**(1), 68–92.

Shakeshaft, C. and Nowell, I. (1984) 'Research on theories, concepts, and models of organizational behavior: The influence of gender' *Issues in Education* **II** (3).

Shakeshaft, C., Nowell, I. and Perry, A. (1991) 'Gender and supervision' *Theory into Practice* **XXX**(2), 134–139.

Tannen, D. (1990) *You Just Don't Understand* New York: Ballentine Books.

Timpano, D. M. and Knight, L. W. (1976) *Sex discrimination — the selection of school district administrators: What can be done?* (NIE Papers — Education and work: Number Three).

Wheatley, M. (1981) 'The impact of organzational structures on issues of sex equity' in Schmuck, P. A., Charters, Jr., W. W. and Carlson, R. O. (eds) *Educational Policy and Management: Sex Differentials* (pp. 255–271) New York: Academic.

5 Towards women-friendly schools

Helen McMullan

The aim of this chapter is to open up the debate as to whether secondary schools could be described as 'women-friendly'. Women enter the teaching profession in large numbers, especially at the primary phase and it remains a popular career path for many at the secondary phase. The question is how open and barrier free are such schools in practice given that women and girls are important 'users' of the system in significant numbers as teachers, learners and parents?

Drawing on a recent study of five secondary schools (three mixed and two single sex) in the same local education authority (LEA), this chapter examines data collected on the current position of women teachers in a sample of about 300 teachers. It is the intention of this chapter to raise questions as to how typical their position is of national practice, what conclusions could be drawn about women in secondary schools in general given this type of current practice as well as how 'friendly' such schools could be for women if there were to be a redress.

Recent national policy changes such as the *Education Reform Act* 1988 (ERA) introduced a National Curriculum, and moves to school self-management (LMS). Such 'radical' change has altered the context in which schools now function on a scale unknown to previous generations of teachers. With the reforms there has been a profound shift in the culture and climate in which schools function and the framework within which women teachers shape and view their careers. There has been a concerted effort on the behalf of national policy makers through change to bring the concepts of 'performance', 'standards', 'choice', 'efficiency', 'effectivess' and 'accountability' to the forefront, leaving a question mark over where exactly the concepts of equity and equality fit into the new framework.

This is not to dispute that the former concepts have never concerned or been important to women teachers. It is however, questionable as to whether the new 'language' and rationality relates to how women regard education, use and practice it as teachers, learners and parents or whether it relates in any way to their current role within it. Are the reforms and associated new 'language' as gender neutral as they may first appear?

The LEA concerned in this particular sample of secondary schools had a high profile for its policies on equality of opportunity. What is questionable is whether such policies extended to the employment of women teachers or whether they had any real influence on the organisation and management practices of secondary schools. There are considerable implications for the employment, training, development and 'careers' of women teachers in the schools within this sample. Despite the apparent existence of policies for equality, questions are left as to the extent that they were taken on board by individual schools.

Changes in national policy may at best mean a consolidation of traditional patterns in which women find themselves marginalised within school hierarchies and therefore from important power and influence over decision-making. At worst the changed educational climate may not have enhanced the position of women and girls in such schools. There is little evidence that there is any real monitoring of women's position by national bodies (other than the unions). Data on women's position in schools is not easily available or accessible and the national picture is certainly unclear.

The radical shift in the resourcing and financing of secondary education combined with economic recession and cuts in public sector spending could have meant that for many schools the management of human resources has become a crude attempt to allocate dwindling or scarce resources amongst both teachers and students. Reform has inevitably shifted responsibility on to schools and when faced with the prospect of an uncertain budget, staffing cuts and redundancy, notions like equality somehow get lost in heated debate. The study reported here revealed that the reality for many women teachers was not necessarily building a career, but maintaining one in a climate more conducive to stagnation than growth or development in real terms. This was evident in the sample of schools below with important implications for women and girls in secondary education. The simple fact remains that reform has introduced an element of discretion into the policy making process at a national and local level in which any real notion of equality can either be taken on board or ignored entirely.

In contrast with primary schools, secondary schools have a long tradition of being largely hierarchical and 'male' centred and orientated. This relates to the fact that few women progress to senior levels and headship. A NUT survey in 1988 found that women teachers were often far less likely to receive incentive allowances (IAs) than their male colleagues and when they did receive them these were often the smallest. The ESRC 'Teachers' Jobs and Lives Project' (Marr, 1991) found women to be a growing 'underclass' of teachers who were remaining unrewarded in schools. In the secondary sector over three per cent of male teachers are heads but for women the figure is well below one per cent. Likewise the career options open to girls once they have left school are far more limited than for boys.

Feminist writers on women in education, for example Acker (1987) and Shakeshaft (1987), have drawn attention to such processes filtering down into the structures of individual schools and classrooms. They raise questions as to the implications for women and girls in those schools which remain without positive, non-stereotyped female role models at senior levels.

Although positive discrimination is not necessarily the answer to women's under-representation (as poor role models can have the opposite effect), feminist writers have vociferously argued that some form of positive action within schools is necessary to remove the barriers to women's development, advancement and roles within the decision-making structures of schools.

What possible future practice may be envisaged to make individual schools more 'friendly' to women and girls given that society generally limits the opportunities available to them? Schools should be 'friendly' in the sense that, given the present climate, women and girls are valued equally alongside men and boys for what they do, who they are and what they have to contribute to the organisation and management of secondary schools. This would mean a move away from traditional hierarchical structures which emphasise individual merit and advancement. This stifles initiative and can create barriers to more democratic forms of organisation based on the principles of collaboration, co-operation and team work which are the styles of organising work and learning that are more 'women-friendly' and are more commonly assumed to suggest flatter structures in which women's concerns begin to be addressed. Schools do not stand alone in bringing about change.

This debate draws on current practice as a 'snapshot' for consideration to view what individual schools could do to give consideration to an element of career structure and development for women teachers with implications for the education of girls; especially in mixed/comprehensive schools.

'Opportunity 2000' was launched in 1991 as part of the 'Business in the Community' initiative. Although 61 companies came forward only eight set themselves numerical targets for the employment and promotion of women. This initiative does signify some level of willingness to tackle the issue but is optional and there is no compulsion on the behalf of employers to look positively at the situation of all female employees. The initiative does not extend to the education service. Rather it considers women entering top positions in the private sector. With the recession there are indications that some employers have had to pull out of the project and it has not been without criticism as a 'token' gesture by the national press.

The study of five schools presented here revealed the importance of the following issues with regard to how women-friendly such schools were in practice:

1. women's concept of career;
2. pay and the developing pattern in the use of discretions, e.g. incentive allowances;
3. subject status and the curriculum;
4. conditions of service;
5. the context of individual school;
6. the management and organisation of a school and the roles of women within responsibility structures;
7. schools individual policies, e.g.
   - development planning,
   - staff development,
   - appraisal,
   - INSET and training,
   - monitoring and evaluation;
8. cost of living factors;
9. marital status, age and length of service;
10. hidden assumptions, attitudes and practices which are unplanned but part of daily practices and relationships.

Women's concept of career

Women's careers are often described using popular stereotypes; broadly summed up as a lack of ambition and commitment. The truth is that women do not necessarily aspire any more or less than men with regard to career development and enhancement, just as girls do not necessarily aspire or view their education any differently than boys do. Feminist debates both within and beyond education would however suggest that depending on how we view circumstances there are processes and practices (overt or covert) which limit the chances and opportunities open to women and girls both within schools and wider society. Women cannot be regarded as a homogenous group but as individuals with their own beliefs, desires, circumstances and aspirations which may or may not coincide with men, with each other or with the organisations in which they spend their working lives. One commonly held belief by feminists is however, that gender itself is the only factor that could explain the persistent lack of power (both financial and positional) held by women in most work organisations and it is therefore the organisation itself that has to answer for this.

Popular explanations to describe women's lack of advancement include:

1. Women and girls do not progress because they do not want to, do not have the confidence, qualifications or abilities. The problem for non-progress is the fault of women and girls themselves.
2. Direct and overt discrimination which results in the exclusion of women and girls through various practices and processes.
3. Covert discrimination through hidden processes and relationships, e.g. stereotyping, use of mentors, networks and sponsors.
4. The notion that organisations are meritocratic and patriarchal, assuming that only the competent succeed and are promoted with the implication that women and girls are not.
5. Organisation, e.g. hierarchy, bureaucracy and hegemony which are the exact opposite of the way women and girls would organise work.
6. The division of labour, i.e. male tasks are more valued than female. The nature of roles and responsibilities, e.g. job descriptions written in a way which directly or indirectly assumes a male. The content of the curriculum is closed to girls but accessible to boys.

To a large extent any one or combination of the above could be operating to the point that women and girls are excluded and denied access to life chances and opportunities which are freely open to males. Although it is argued that this also depends on the 'conceptual lens' which is being used to justify and explain why women and girls remain in these positions.

There is evidence to suggest that within the present educational climate, individual schools and the policies of heads and governors take sole responsibility for creating or stifling any prospect or notion of career within a school. It is in the best interest of schools that governors produce sound policies on staff development and on pay. It rests with individual heads and governors to create a fair system of reward which is informed by a perspective on equality and which establishes structures that enable men and women to take an equal share and responsibility for decision-making in the best interests of all students. This is not going to be easy for many as inequality is so deeply ingrained in the management practices of many secondary schools. Fears have been expressed as to the practices of 'lay' governors in making decisions not just about pay, but of promotion and appointment procedures. This would further reduce the chances of women gaining senior posts in schools as preferences for men over women continue to predominate.

Creating a culture in which teachers perceive any sense of career in a school extends well beyond who gets which incentive allowances and why, what promotional prospects exist in a school, or how much training is available and how it is delivered. It extends to the prevailing ethos and culture of a school through decision-making, management practices and processes, leadership style of the head, and the way in which resources are administered, organised and allocated within a school. The restructuring of education through the reforms has created a situation where there is no longer a sense of uniformity of practice or expectations, either within or between schools.

Traditional concepts of a 'career' often present it as a conscious and deliberate attempt to progress through the hierarchy. In this sense the concept of a career is often an 'objective' notion which relates to the rational structures of an organisation. Career is often defined in rational terms, e.g. that hierarchy, prestige, continuity and upward mobility are prime motivators as this is the culture of a particular school. Writers and researchers in the field of education, i.e. Acker (1987), Ball and Goodson (1985) and Goodson (1992) refer to the more 'subjective' aspects, e.g. there are deeply personal aspects of teachers' work which makes it very distinctive from other types of work. Ball (1987) describes career as 'political' and about 'struggles over the definition of the school'.

There are also widely held beliefs that women do not necessarily perceive career in the traditional way that men do simply because of the importance they place on relationships in order to achieve objectives (Shakeshaft 1987). The term 'career' needs to be broadened to include women's concept of it. Contemporary feminists (Wolfe 1990, Coward 1992) emphasise the above. Coward's research into the lives of 'successful' career women has a critical edge. Her women were found to be 'giving up' on making demands at work simply because of what being 'career orientated' means to women. She describes the concept of 'trial by personality' i.e. that for many women progression through the hierarchy involves 'pitting' yourself against another person as a person. This she claims is not a process which men go through in seeking promotion or in pursuing a career. Many of the women studied by Coward had retreated away from work or given it up entirely (by lapsing into marriage and childrearing), through the sheer frustration of not 'fitting in'. This had to do with the disillusionment experienced by women as male bosses and co-workers failed to establish a work ethos and culture that both men and women aspired to/went along with.

Studies of women within education (Riches 1990, Torrington and Weightman 1989) have also found that despite gaining progress and obtaining influential leadership positions women face isolation, criticism of their leadership style and lack of support simply because of the way in which 'competence' is defined in 'masculine' terms. The whole notion of 'competence' has certainly created fear for women in the schools under consideration as they felt that male managers would not be objective in appraising and assessing what women do, although this was also compounded by divisions in subject status explored below.

Pay

Although the *Equal Pay Act* (1961) created legal protection for women there is little to suggest the extent to which this has affected the position of women teachers. Some legal action has begun to reach the courts and media attention; but it is not extensive. Teachers' pay has been the subject of continued debate and change by national policy makers. The shape of the changes to teachers' pay indicates a desire on the behalf of national policy makers to assess schools more through the 'performance' of teachers.

The School Teacher's Review Body (STRB) stated that the intentions of the pay structure are primarily to aid recruitment, retention and motivation of teachers. There is no evidence that pay alone affects any of these. There is an emphasis in the report that this specifically refers to 'quality' teachers; a term which in itself is open to interpretation and difficult to define simply because of the nature of teachers' work. There is an element of frustration in the report that 'there are no clear, universally agreed measures of good teaching'.

As individual schools pay policies begin to take shape under the auspicies of the new 'pay and conditions document 1992' and governors begin to exercise discretion over pay, questions need to be asked about what effect this new 'performance' culture is going to have on teachers and especially on women, particularly since the new pay structure is geared to the 'selective' identification and reward of 'quality' teachers to which there is considerable discretion. This emphasis is a recipe for inequality as previous practice has shown.

There has been continued interest by national policy makers (Tomlinson, 1992) in performance related pay (PRP) or merit pay. *DES Circular 8/92* (p.13) states that:

> Successful schools of the future will be those which use their pay discretions purposefully and selectively to strengthen manangement structures, recruit and retain staff of the highest quality and reward achievement in the classroom . . . they need to draw on a variety of sources of information including relevant information from appraisal.

How individual heads and governors use their discretion over pay still remains to be seen but there are important implications for women in this.

A glimpse at the five secondary schools studied shows how the new pay structure is working in practice in a sample of schools. It reveals more about the types of extended hierarchies which some secondary schools are now developing and of the operation of pay discretions for individual teachers and for women.

The five schools were chosen at random to represent the range of schools within the LEA. They are fairly representative of schools in this location, which has a mixed multiracial school population.

Table 5.1 shows the actual number of teachers benefitting from the incentive allowance (IA) structure. What becomes apparent is that IAs are increasingly being used to create both gender divisions in rewards and promote the hierarchical nature of the schools in practice through an eight tier promotional structure. Forty four per cent of men are paid on scale 'D' or above compared to 18 per cent of women.

Table 5.1

	MPG	A	B	C	D	E	DH	HD	Total
Male	45	5	26	8	37	16	10	3	150
Female	58	18	25	21	15	5	4	2	148

The DES (1992) states that the 'relevant body' may award such allowances in accordance with the following criteria:

1. If a teacher 'undertakes responsibilities beyond those common to the majority of teachers'.
2. If a teacher demonstrates 'outstanding ability as a classroom teacher'.
3. If a teacher is 'employed to teach subjects in which there is a shortage of teachers'.
4. Employment to a post which is difficult to fill.

Although the language is 'gender neutral' practice reveals that gender is becoming more significant than would be assumed in the above criteria. Evidence from the schools under consideration shows that in practice IAs are being awarded purely for responsibility, subject and value of a subject or a responsibility and not extensively for any other purpose. Table 5.1 shows that although there are roughly equal numbers of men and women in posts there exists what appears to be two parallel 'opportunity structures' within this hierarchy. For women this simply results in a situation in which the majority of women remain at and below IA 'C' and at the lower IA levels.

The allocation of allowances to men however, reveals a far less consistent pattern of rewards, suggesting that not only are men far more likely to be awarded IAs but they are also two to three times more likely to be obtaining the higher IAs than women.

Whilst the School Teachers Review Body states a figure of 65 per cent of teachers holding IAs, this particular sample showed that in practice this varied across the schools from 52 per cent to 69 per cent. The percentage of men and women gaining promoted posts was far more significant. Men were far more likely to gain promotion than women. At the higher IA levels men were two to three times more likely than women to be obtaining allowances for posts.

On the whole women were doing far better in the single sex girls school and in schools with female rather than male heads. In the case of schools with female heads women tended to remain at the school for a much longer period of time than elsewhere.

The above situation was similar for black teachers who were generally less likely to be obtaining IAs but more likely to be obtaining higher IAs in schools where the head was female or black than in others.

The use of IAs to create an opportunity structure within the schools revealed that no consistent patterns could be identified and there was no uniformity of practice for posts of responsibility between the schools.

It was at middle management level that the use of discretion over pay was particularly marked in the schools studied. Middle management was very often denoted by the use of IA 'C' and 'D'. Women were more likely to be awarded an IA 'C' for a post of responsibility at middle management than were men who were frequently more likely to be awarded an IA 'D' for such a role.

The award of IAs had no relationship to the number of responsibilities actually being carried. There was evidence to suggest that women were frequently carrying more responsibilities than men for a lower IA, e.g. a 'C' rather than a 'D'. On the basis of this evidence it appears as though a value is also being placed on the nature of responsibility and the gender of the post holder rather than purely on the amount of responsibility. This would seem to suggest that the work of women teachers is valued less than that of men.

The use of pay in the above ways is particularly unfriendly to women. Recent emphasis on PRP, if widely adopted, could prove to further disadvatage women. American examples showed that early usage of PRP was 'divisive' and did not necessarily improve the performance of schools. Such schemes were abandoned as they discouraged co-operation, the sharing of job knowledge, increased the unfair allocation of awards through 'favouritism', led to poor morale and increased staff dissension and jealousy (Johnson 1984).

The use of pay at the level of individual schools should monitored more closely by governors and heads who should consider the gender implications of pay discretions. Schools that consider the use of pay in shaping management structures rather than only valuing subject and status will be able to offer careers to all.

Valuing and rewarding all staff both financially and through conditions of service are set to become factors which teachers will be attracted by and schools would be wise to make this aspect a 'selling' point to recruit and retain good teachers who may be in a position to move away from schools which prove to be 'bad employers' in this and other respects.

Subject status and the National Curriculum

Subject qualifications have become a significant factor in the award and value of pay discretions in the schools studied. Table 5.2 shows the distribution by gender of teachers to the various curricular areas.

Table 5.2

Subject	Gender	
	M %	F %
English	39	61
Maths	73	27
Science	68	32
Technology	65	35
Business education	50	50
Humanities	75	25
Languages	34	66
Arts	49	51
Special needs	21	79

From the table an obvious subject hierarchy became evident in the schools surveyed and there is a clear gender basis to this. Only business studies had no bias. Maths, science, technology and Humanities were predominantly male and formed a major part of the core curriculum. These subjects were also areas where men were gaining a significant number of the higher IAs.

English, languages, arts and special needs were predominantly female and with the exception of English were not a significant part of the core curriculum of the schools. These subjects also carried far fewer higher value IAs.

Table 5.3 summarises the percentage of IAs allocated across all schools by gender. On the basis of this evidence teachers of maths, science, technology and humanities stood a far greater chance of gaining promotion. These were curricular areas that had a particularly high number of men gaining the higher IAs. In sharp contrast, languages, arts and special needs carried few of the higher value allowances and were predominantly female.

Table 5.3

IA	C %	D %	E %	Total
'Male' subjects				
Men	11.4	59.1	29.5	44
Women	56.2	31.3	12.5	16
Overall	23.3	51.6	25.0	60
'Female' subjects				
Men	14.3	64.2	21.4	14
Women	40.9	45.4	13.6	22
Overall	30.5	52.8	16.7	36

The table shows the contrast between the allowances gained by men and women. More 'E' allowances were evident in 'male' subjects in contrast with 'female' subjects (25 per cent as opposed to 17 per cent). It was also clear that men were doing far better in both 'male' and 'female' subjects.

Although it is not clear just how typical this sample is of existing practice nationally a subject hierarchy is developing in which men are gaining a significant advantage over women with regard to higher, allowances for certain key subjects. Women however predominated in curricular areas which received fewer of the higher value allowances and they were almost devalued in the process by having the least value attached to them.

More women friendly schools would see a more even distribution of IAs irrespective of the subject or the gender of individuals. Of particular concern is the gender division on the basis of subject. Why the schools have chosen to allocate so many high IAs to men in particular subjects is questionable if it is merely for responsibility for a particular subject area. With regard to higher value IAs being awarded for additional responsibility in addition to subject, it is questionable as to the effects of having management practices in which the managers management all share a particular area of the curriculum or are from a similar discipline. The ethos in which women from other subject areas are not reaching senior management is surely to the disadvantage of the school and its ability to change.

Conditions of service

The 'School Teacher's Pay and Conditions Document 1992' relates largely to pay and only 20 per cent of the document relates to conditions of service. With the exception of specifying the professional duties and responsibilities of teachers and senior managers, cover arrangements, the 1,265 hours and five other INSET days, the document says little about the actual quality of working life in schools. This has been picked up and intensively researched by the unions.

Research by AMMA–Warwick University found workloads of teachers to be increasing dramatically as a result of the practical requirements of implementing major aspects of education reforms. Class sizes were found to be increasing whilst non-contact time had decreased. AMMA found that there had been an average increase in workloads of as much as five hours for some Year 2 teachers, some of whom were found to be working a 72 hour week with increasing workloads. In addition they found administrative loads increasing without equivalent technical or administrative support.

In 'The Workloads of Secondary School Teachers', AMMA found there were particular gender implications in the changes made to teachers' work. Women were found to be disadvantaged in comparison with their male colleagues; teaching larger classes, clustered on the lower salary levels and found to be more likely to be on fixed term contracts than men. On the whole women were found to be working longer hours and considered to be cheaper. In referring to women as an 'exploited group of workers' they recommended that governors look more closely into the pay and conditions of women.

It is the conditions of work which are particularly important in affecting the quality of work, morale and therefore learning in schools. National policy makers have assumed that quantitative indicators such as pay alone is what motivates teachers. There is no evidence to suggest this. The quality of working life in schools has been lost in the debate and it is women teachers who are losing out.

The context of individual schools

All of the schools in this study served a mixed, multiracial community. There was evidence to suggest that with regard to teachers the schools with larger numbers of students were creating more posts with higher IAs. In addition such schools were more likely to have a more clearly defined management structure. The opposite was true of schools with smaller numbers of students or with falling rolls where there was no coherent management structure. In these schools there were large discrepancies in the award and value of IAs and subject and gender divisions were more obvious. Although it was common practice for a head of faculty to be awarded an IA 'D', in the schools with higher numbers of students some heads of faculties were awarded IA 'E', but the same post would be an IA 'C' in a smaller school.

There is further a great deal of debate as to what constitutes 'outstanding performance' and how it can be quantified. Saran (1992) questions:

> . . . how performance in a caring profession can be assessed qualitatively let alone quantitively, since productivity is such an elusive concept when a service like education is compared with the output of manufacturing industry.

The management and organisation of schools and the roles of women within them

The research into school effectiveness and school improvement would suggest that the improvement and development of schools rests not only with individuals but with the whole school working together towards shared goals. The collegial nature of teaching appears to have been overlooked in the development of the types of hierarchies outlined above. These frequently led to a situation in which women were confined to particular subject areas and to lower status posts of responsibility carrying lower value IAs. Only in one of the schools was the middle management more equally rewarded in terms of IAs. There are considerable implications for this particular type of arrangement: women's influence over important management decisions was very limited.

There is nothing in the legislation that compels schools to organise themselves in the ways outlined above, with the hierarchies based on subject, some responsibilities but not others or historical factors. The exclusion of women from senior levels is surely not beneficial to the education of all students or for decision-making within it.

The schools under consideration here showed clearly that women were largely in stereotyped roles, either because these were the only opportunities open to them or because there was a reluctance to appoint women to certain posts. One particular gender division was the pastoral/academic division. With the exception of one school the majority of heads of year were women and heads of faculty men, although there was evidence to suggest that the division was also financial as heads of year were often paid on lower IAs than heads of faculty. In the largest school where pastoral and academic posts were given similar allowances the academic posts were predominantly occupied by men leaving women in pastoral roles.

Male dominated hierarchies do little for women entering the profession. These women will be a generation of teachers without the role models to influence or support them with implications for the future education of girls.

Schools' individual policies

If women largely occupy the lower levels of the school's hierarchy there are tremendous implications with regard to planning, INSET needs, training and appraisal.

One noticeable practice that could be identified in the above schools was the ill-defined role of staff development. With the exception of the girls' school there was no obvious policy for equal opportunities with regard to development, training or INSET.

With the changed inspection framework and the declining role of the LEA advisors there is a question mark over aspects of 'support' for schools and for women teachers. There is clearly a need for training, INSET and career counselling as modes of support and this will not necessarily be supplied at the level of the LEA. Given the evidence here, schools will have to address seriously these aspects with regard to their internal management practices, especially if women are not to continue to miss out on experiences required for promotion or professional development. An emphasis on 'development' rather than purely 'appraisal' which provides a level of support with access to training, INSET, time for courses and professional development is going to be much needed in schools. Practice would suggest that this is missing.

Unlike industry and the business world (who frequently have a 'personnel' department), schools will have to look seriously at their responsibility to provide a 'woman-friendly' career structure. Stated targets for the employment of women teachers, their development, training and regard to monitoring and evaluation might help their progress. Structures which deny access to training and development to women are likely to hinder the progress and ethos of individual schools; especially those which are mixed and/or multiracial.

Cost of living and external factors

Economic recession and the changed role of women in society have a bearing on teachers in many ways. It can no longer be assumed that women teachers all marry and use their earnings to subsidise that of their husbands. This and other similar myths about women have been explored in great detail by contemporary feminists (Coward 1992, Wolfe 1990).

Many women remain the sole breadwinner and can even be single parents or supporting sick relatives or partners who are unemployed. Childcare arrangements and maternity arrangements are two large questions which need to be looked into by school governors and heads. Attractive packages will have to be offered to women if the service is to retain able women teachers. This would include concepts such as flexible work hours, an increase in the number of part-time posts on higher IAs, job share schemes which extend to all levels of the hierarchy, child care arrangements and nursery provision; there are examples of a few areas where schools will have to consider the attractive, competitive terms and conditions offered in other types of work such as nursery places and other non-pay benefits.

Marital status, age and length of service

Shakeshaft (1987) found that many career orientated women in education found that the demands of work and marriage were incompatible. This particular aspect is also explored by contemporary feminists, e.g. (1990) Wolfe and Coward (1992). There is very little research as to the extent that this influences women in schools but it was a factor for some women in senior posts in the schools surveyed.

Longevity of service was certainly a factor in the distribution of the higher IA post holders but this was more likely to affect men than women. Even more significant was the impact of the gender of headteachers on women's willingness to remain at a school for a lengthy period of time, i.e. beyond two to three years. In the schools with female heads women tended to have remained at the school for longer periods of time than at those with male heads.

Hidden assumptions

It would be wise policy for schools to evaluate the effects of practices and procedures on the way women and girls experience schools. The emphasis in the sample schools on hierarchies which largely reward men and place a greater value on their roles in relation to women has many implications for daily practice.

Conclusions

The concept of 'career' is now more widely affected by the decisions, attitudes and priorities of senior managers and in the way that resources, INSET, appraisal and development are managed. 'Women friendly' schools would therefore be those schools in which the decision-making processes are informed by an awareness of equality and equity. It is clear that a good appraisal system will be vital in schools but this should focus on development and improvement of schools. It will be to the disadvantage of schools if they fail to harness the talents of all staff in decision-making and development and those which do not address the forms of disadvantage experienced by female teachers. This could mean a radical shift in the way schools regard managing the 'personnel function' from recruitment, selection and induction to training, development, career planning and counselling in addition to promotion. It is not going to be easy for many secondary schools to move from hierarchical structures to flatter structures which emphasise democratic decision-making. As this study revealed the importance of teams and co-operation is presently alien to the way many schools currently function. Men may have much to learn from 'women-friendly' schools.

References

Acker, J. (1987) *Teachers, Gender and Careers* Lewes: Falmer.
AMMA (1991) *AMMA Evidence to the School Teacher's Review Body* London: AMMA.
Ball, S. J. (1987) *The Micropolitics of the School* London: Routledge and Kegan Paul.
Ball, S. J. and Goodson (1985) *Teachers' Lives and Careers* Lewes: Falmer.
Coopers, Lybrand and Deloitte/NFER (1992) *LMS Initiative; a Study into Formulae Funding and Management Issues* Slough: NFER.
Coward, R. (1992) *Our Treacherous Hearts* London: Faber and Faber.
DES (1992) *Schoolteachers' Pay and Conditions Document 1992* London: HMSO.
DES (1992) *Schoolteachers' Pay and Conditions of Employment* Circulars No. 8/92 & Circular No. 10/91, London: HMSO.
Goodson, I. (1992) *Studying Teachers' Lives* London: Routledge.
Johnson, S. M. (1984) 'Merit pay for teachers: a poor prescription for reform' in *Harvard Educational Review* **54**, (2) May.
Marr, A. (1991) 'Changes to Improve The Quality of Education: Teachers' Perceptions' Draft Report to ESRC.
Riches C. (1989) *Gender and School Management* in Saran R. and Trafford U. *Research in Education Management and Policy* Lewes: Falmer.
Saran, R. (1992) *The History of Teachers' Pay Negotiations* in Tomlinson, H. (ed) (1992) *Performance-Related Pay in Education London:* Routledge.
School Teachers' Review Body (1992) *First Report* London: HMSO.
Shakeshaft, C. (1987) *Women School Administrators* Sage.
Tomlinson, H. (1992) *Performance Related Pay in Education* London: Routledge
Torrington, D. and Weightman, J. (1989) *The Reality of School Management* Blackwell Education.
Wolfe, N. (1990) *The Beauty Myth* London: Chatto and Windus.

6 'Women-friendly' management development programmes

Anne Gold

Introduction

The provision of programmes for teachers who are managers in educational institutions makes up a large part of the activity at the Management Development Centre at the Institute of Education in London. The Centre was set up in 1984, and has gone through several changes: in name, in character, and in staffing, since then. Our work in the particular area of encouraging women into education management became an intentional undertaking after we realised that we had been addressing it in a less consciously planned way for some time. Our work in this area had been developing over several years, and is borne out by the fact that the ratio of women to men on our programmes compares well with the ratio of women to men in teaching, (Ouston, Gold and Gosling 1992), although men are in the majority in the *management* of education in this country (Al-Khalifa 1989).

In 1990, our Management Development Centre changed from a centre staffed predominantly by women to one staffed almost exclusively by women. At the same time, a woman senior inspector in a local education authority pointed out that the introduction of the local management of schools seemed to be deterring women from applying for senior management posts in education. She suggested that we might think about running a development programme to encourage women into educational management.

During the preceding two years, we had become aware that we were developing a particular style in the way we ran our management programmes, and were concerned that the style should be evident in our publicity material and in our course descriptions. Previously we had been working with some programme participants who felt that our way of developing management skills experientially was not compatible with their expectations of a more didactic course. So from 1990 onwards, we tried to develop a 'house style' in our publicity, with careful descriptions of the way we work. Since then, we have had fewer arguments about teaching methods, and at the same time more women have taken part in our programmes generally. At some stage, we know that we would like to explore whether this is because women are more attracted to the style of learning we offer.

Management Development Centre programmes

For the last two years, I have been working particularly closely with Beryl Husain, an ex-ILEA comprehensive school headteacher, to develop and deliver management programmes at the Management Development Centre. In all our Centre programmes now, we are concerned particularly with the professional development of adults who are usually already professionally effective. Almost all our work is with teachers whose classroom experience has led them to make the decision to become managers in education, usually from a base of good classroom practice. The teachers we work with already have a strong sense of their professional selves as classroom teachers with a body of knowledge and experience which defines those selves. We work with them to 're-professionalise' themselves into managers, by helping them to reframe a new body of knowledge and experience as educational managers. In North America, the first task that assistant principals (the equivalent of deputy headteachers) must undertake in socialising themselves into becoming school administrators is to decide 'to leave teachers and teaching behind' (Marshall, 1992). We often have discussions in our programmes that are begun by teachers with management responsibilities who are reluctant to give up their teaching responsibilities. We think that it is important to acknowledge that becoming a manager means working with other adults to ensure that the teaching and learning in a school is effective. They should not leave 'teachers and teaching behind', therefore, but should not necessarily do the teaching themselves.

In Britain, it is difficult to gain promotion without evidence of long experience and deep understanding of the classroom skills that lead to valid learning, and without at least a basic understanding of the organisational structure of educational establishments. Many of our participants are already skilled managers who come to us either to confirm or to extend their skills. Often their comments at the end of our programmes show that their most important learning has been that they 'were doing it right anyway'. Most teachers lack confidence about their work, and the attacks on education during the last decade have compounded their lack of confidence. As learning facilitators, we often find ourselves involved in a process of confirming then extending good practice.

Our task is rarely, therefore, to persuade our participants that management is a necessary activity, or even to explore basic ideas about the ethics and processes of management, except as a starting point for more profound explorations. Rather, we embed in our programmes notions of self-development through reflection on practice, by offering frameworks and programme-based experiences to make sense of their work-based experience. Much of our work, especially when developing the interpersonal skills most necessary for effective management, involves experiential learning.

Burnard (1989) identifies the stages of experiential learning:

> 1. personal experience;
> 2. reflection on that experience;
> 3. the transformation of knowledge and meaning as a result of that reflection.
>
> A fourth stage, in which we use what we have learned, may also be added to the first three and thus a continuous cycle of experience–reflection–transformation of knowledge and meaning–action (experience), is created. (p. 3)

We realised that our work resonates with Kolb's (1984) cycle of experiential learning, particularly because we are working with professionally experienced adults:

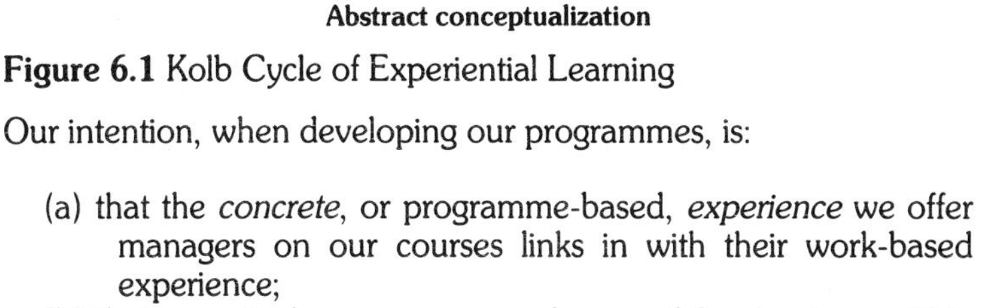

Figure 6.1 Kolb Cycle of Experiential Learning

Our intention, when developing our programmes, is:

(a) that the *concrete*, or programme-based, *experience* we offer managers on our courses links in with their work-based experience;

(b) that our actual programmes, and some of the structures within them that we offer, provide an arena for *reflective observation*;

(c) that the frameworks we are able to offer, placed as we are within a university and more able to be in touch with current research than people based in schools, are a form of *abstract conceptualization;*

(d) and that the modular shape of most of our programmes allows participants the opportunity to use the newly framed knowledge in planning or *active experimentation* back at work.

Most of our programmes are nine days long. We offer them in three modules of three days each, with a month between each module. Participants often comment on the way they come to feel that the programmes last a term, not just nine days, because the thinking and learning between the modules is sustained by the times back at the Centre. And the thinking and learning at the Centre is sustained by the times back at work. We are very careful to link the Centre and the school-based work in order to maximise the continuous and cyclical nature of the learning.

Let us look in more detail at the way the four stages of experiential learning are built into our programmes.

Concrete experience

We build several sessions of concrete experience through experiential learning and role play into our programmes, sometimes very explicitly, and sometimes acknowledged afterwards in the review of the sessions. We have learnt over the years that all experiential learning, especially with adults, has to be planned for and handled very carefully.

Teachers' understanding of learning processes, and of the discomfort but the necessity of risk-taking leads them to be sceptical of 'games' as a basis for learning. Although important group processes can be revealed through 'content free' activities, we understand their scepticism. Hence, most of the concrete experiences we offer during the programmes are fairly obviously directly relevant to the participants' work-based experiences.

We try to make risk-taking as safe but productive as possible. We begin the programmes sensitively and carefully, with ice-breakers and introductions, and with a negotiated contract, which has become central to the way we work. After explaining the way we work, including the group work and the experiential work, we ask participants to brainstorm what they need from each other in order to feel safe enough to take risks. The brainstorm is then refined so that everyone can agree to it, and it is put up on the wall at the front of the room for the rest of the course. At the beginning and end of each day, the facilitators ask whether anyone has any comments about the contract. A silence grows as people read through it, and often they begin to allude to it throughout the day. In some courses, it has become a focal point, with choruses of 'Contract!' when people think that it has been broken. Brookfield (1986), writes about a climate for learning:

> in which adults can feel free to challenge one another and can feel comfortable with being challenged . . . the honest expression of differences in an atmosphere where challenge and dissension are accepted as part of the educational process. (p. 13)

We have been encouraged by our course members to refine the language describing the experiential tasks we set so that as many of them as possible feel included in the task. Previously, we were shown several times that our lack of attention to issues of equal opportunities allowed a gender bias to show in our instructions. For example, for several years we have begun our team building sessions with a task called 'construct an object'. The instructions initially read:

> Construct an object of maximum height, length and elegance.

We have provided a variety of materials at different times, sometimes wood and string, and sometimes coloured crepe paper and straws, and we have changed the wording of the instructions several times as a result of feedback from women participants who felt excluded from the task. The most productive set of instructions, which has allowed most people to take part, has proved to be:

> As a team, with the available material, construct an object of maximum elegance, portability and usefulness.

We do not know why the change in language has had gender specific results, but we changed the wording of the task in response to suggestions from women who were not involved in the task, and now we do not see women unable to take part in it. We are still experimenting with materials, but find that the more colourful they are, the more motivated people are to take part, the more fun people have, and the more effective is the learning about the working of teams. This task is used as a way of exploring how groups of people become teams, and work together to achieve a task. We follow it up, after an observer's session, with a theoretical input about team roles, and a handout about team role inventories, which is usually Belbin's team role inventory.

Brookfield (1986) writes:

> The notion of praxis as alternating and continuous engagements by teachers and learners in exploration, action, and reflection is central to adult learning. It means that explorations of new ideas, skills, or bodies

> of knowledge do not take place in a vacuum but are set within the context of learners' past, current and future experiences. (p. 15)

Weil and McGill (1989) and Boud and Feletti (1991) also write about the importance of attaching the frameworks of the learning to the professional experience of the learners. They show that adults learn better when they can understand the reality and validity of the learning activities they are involved in. They write that valuing the prior experience of adult professional learners offers a very useful resource for further learning.

In our work at the Centre, acknowledging the professional experience of the participants holds another equally important function: previous experience is validated by the references to it, and raised to a level of importance unacknowledged by the participants themselves. They were just 'doing' the work themselves as part of their job, not really understanding the skill with which they did it, not understanding the transferable nature of most of the skills from classroom to managing, or the high level of interpersonal skills they were employing when managing with people.

There seems to be a link between our acknowledgement of the professional skills and the careful framing of them within the programmes, and the level of confidence built up by our work. Perhaps this is why we regularly comment on the numerous references to 'confidence' and 'I now understand I was doing it right already' that we read in our course evaluations, and that I referred to at the beginning of this chapter.

And are we particularly answering the professional development needs of women by working this way? Daryl Agnew (1989) in reviewing her courses for women found:

> Time and again women referred to the need to 'develop greater self-confidence' and 'help with my career development' as being major factors in choosing the course. (p. 75)

If this is so, it must be particularly important for the women and men on our programmes who are trapped within the patriarchal nature of our society, and who see the interpersonal skills they employ so effectively denied their specialness. In this case recognising and endorsing those skills within the validation of their previous professional experience both serves to anchor the newly offered frameworks into a recognisable reality, and empowers the learners in a way which affects all their practice.

Reflective observation

Schön (1987) would describe the work done at the Centre as 'the reflective practicum' which takes place within a 'professional school', thus placing most importance on the reflective nature of the activity:

> My design for a coherent professional school places a reflective practicum at the center, as a bridge between the worlds of university and practice. (p. 309)

In his reflective practicum, he echoes Brookfield's climate of learning, giving responsibility to us, the programme designers or 'coaches', to:

> include values and norms conducive to reciprocal, public reflection on understandings and feelings usually kept private and tacit . . . [the coaches] must cultivate activities that connect the knowing- and reflection-in-action of competent practitioners to the theories and techniques taught as professional knowledge in academic courses. (p. 311–312)

The tasks we introduce as concrete experiences in the programmes are followed by *group discussions* which encourage 'reflection-in-action'. For several years, we were aware that many programmes set up for teachers which use small group work and workshops, gather all the participants together into a plenary session to report back on the activities in the small groups. These sessions can be very tedious, particularly when several groups report back consecutively. They are either repetitious, or they are full of references which mean a great deal to the small group, but very little to the larger one. They were often dominated by the most confident men who had been nominated by their groups to report back, and the less confident people who felt intimidated by the group remained silent.

For the learning from the completion of the task to be most effective, a directed discussion which helped them to draw conclusions from their experiences, led by the coach or facilitator, was necessary. We now begin our whole group sessions after small group tasks with such questions as:

- Was that a useful exercise?
- If not, why not?
- If it was, why?
- What did you learn from it?

The atmosphere in many of these discussions is creative, intensive, and powerful. It seems to us that it is important that suggestions and contributions are accepted in a non-judgemental manner. It is often at this point in the programme that the contract becomes activated, and the groups that have internalised it most successfully listen to each other with respect, interest and mutual support. Brookfield's 'atmosphere where challenge and dissension are accepted as part of the educational process' is most palpable here. He explains very clearly why these sessions can be so powerful:

> Facilitation aims to foster in adults a spirit of critical reflection. Through educational encounters, learners come to appreciate that values, beliefs, behaviours, and ideologies are culturally transmitted and that they are provisional and relative. This awareness that the supposed givens of work conduct, relationships, and political allegiances are, in fact, culturally constructed means that adults will come to question many aspects of their professional, personal, and political lives. (p. 11)

We often see people struggling to make sense and a coherence out of their professional experiences during these group discussions. There is evidence of the beginnings of changes in attitudes, and of challenges to long-held assumptions.

The facilitator combines the suggestions and conclusions from the participants with references to research and writings for those who are interested to follow up with reading. Sometimes, handouts summarising the research findings are given out at this point. These mean much more to the participants because they are clear explanations of the experiences actually worked through within the small groups.

However, we often find that our own prepared handouts are superfluous at this point. Our understanding of adult learning (and indeed all learning) leads us to write down the summaries of the learning as it arises, as well as to verbalise them, allowing learners time to think, and different ways to understand the learning. Hence, we list the most important learning points raised in the discussions on flipcharts in front of the group. We are often struck by the quality of these lists, and we either reproduce them for participants, or leave them accessible till the end of the programme.

Another interesting outcome has been that because of the tentative, reflective and experimental nature of most of the discussion, almost all members of the large group take part. It becomes obvious that all suggestions and contributions are welcome — there is not one correct answer. Because participants experiment with ideas and make suggestions as they talk, it becomes clear that speaking hesitatingly, slowly and thoughtfully, and framing sentences while speaking is acceptable. So those people who will only speak when they have perfectly formed sentences learn to take risks with their coherence. The facilitators are prepared to wait for responses, feeling at ease with silences while those involved in the discussion organise their thoughts. It seems to me that women particularly have felt liberated by this method of working. They certainly refer to the discussions in their evaluations of the programme as giving them confidence and letting them understand that they have something important to offer.

As many questions are raised as are answered during these sessions, and we often acknowledge that as with all experiential learning, answers arise sometimes unexpectedly at different phases of the cycle of learning. It is a very important part of the learning process, however, to frame the correct question.

We also encourage *individual* reflection. We give all participants a professional journal in which we suggest they reflect privately on the programme as it proceeds. We produce a new journal for each programme, and include in it the title and dates of each module, our aims, and three questions to be addressed individually at the beginning of each module:

- What would you like to gain from this course?
- What might stop you from gaining it?
- What will help you to achieve it?

We then leave space for initial reactions to each session and for further reflections. We suggest that participants fill these in each evening, and often see them writing in them during the day. At the end of each module we leave a whole page for them to write about the learning they would like to take back to work.

We see this journal as serving at least two purposes. The first is to encourage regular private reflection in what can be a very active and busy nine days. We hope that this models practice that our participants will endeavour to introduce back at work. Many of our senior managers come to us with high levels of stress and work overload. An encouragement to build time for reflection into their day, however brief it may be, relieves them of feelings of guilt about not 'doing' or performing all the time.

And we hope that the questions in the journal encourage participants to take charge of their own learning. Even in adulthood, too many people see learning as something that is imposed on them, rather than something that they may have control over. Although we publish our course aims and objectives, we encourage a certain amount of negotiated learning, both within modules and in the project writing. The negotiation and the questions about individual needs for effective learning ensure that the learners are actively involved in shaping their own learning.

Abstract conceptualisation

We have already begun to explore the 'answer seeking' part of the cycle within the 'question asking' part of the reflective observation mode. David Jaques (1991) divides this part of the cycle into two:

— interpreting, making sense of data,
and
— generalizing, developing hypotheses and principles. (p. 10)

I welcome Jaques' division here, because it clarifies a problem for me. *Who* interprets and makes sense of the data? *Who* generalizes and develops hypotheses and principles? Effective learning involves the learner fully, and therefore suggests a very active part in finding answers. But learners are also conditioned to look to their 'teachers' for answers. As university teachers, we are often seen ambivalently. Our learners expect us to have an academic framework that they do not normally have access to, with all the answers, but they also mistrust some of the answers because they do not see university teachers as practitioners.

In planning our programmes we try to find the balance between offering hypotheses based on research findings in a didactic, lecture-type mode, and leaving it entirely to participants to make sense of the data themselves. Making the shift between being a receptive facilitator and an information giving lecturer is sometimes difficult. But it is an important balance, and most of the time, we think that we work in the way described by Brookfield (1986):

> Facilitation is collaborative. Facilitators and learners are engaged in a co-operative enterprise in which, at different times and for different purposes, leadership and facilitation roles will be assumed by different group members. (p. 10)

We vary the ways we suggest hypotheses, sometimes offering them before a group task which then tests them out, sometimes drawing them up together with our participants in the discussions after a group task, and sometimes offering research findings that allow participants to draw up their own hypotheses.

Some years ago, we used to invite guest speakers as experts. But since we have developed our more experiential programmes, our participants are often dissatisfied with the 'experts' inputs. It seems that the more intensive the learning experience, the more important it is that the teaching style 'fits' the whole programme. There are also problems here with the notion of expertise. Many of our participants are experts in their field. They look less often to us to provide the hypotheses and more often to us to provide the framework for them to frame hypotheses *themselves.*

We are, however, part of a university, with access to an academic library and to research. We are aware that several of our participants choose our programmes because of our academic links. Recently we have been experimenting with the most satisfactory method of opening up access to relevant literature. When we sent people book lists before the beginning of our programmes, they had no time to read and came to us believing themselves to be failures already. When we gave them book lists at the beginning of the programmes, they were so busy networking with each other and establishing contacts that they did not have time to visit the library. Now we give them a book list at the beginning of the programme, but we also put a selection of relevant books in the main room where we work, so that people can glance through them to select books which resonate with their personal learning style. We offer the references and the literature, but we leave it to the participants to choose what use they make of them.

Active experimentation

Our reading of the report of the School Management Task Force (1990) encouraged us to formalise this part of the cycle more carefully. The School Management Task Force suggested that management development should take place much more on-site than previously. It wrote that those people who are planning to develop further their management skills should do so within their own schools or consortium of schools:

> A major argument for a new approach is that management development must deal more realistically with the problem of access to support than the current course-driven model can. (p.4).
> Training programmes for heads should have a similar form to other school management training, with the emphasis moving away from residential sessions, heavily dependent on speakers, towards self-directed study, using distance learning materials and information packs and working on projects or personal management skills, often with other members of the management team, to improve the total management performance of the school. (p. 19)

Several years ago when I taught in schools, it seemed to me that some teachers sat in staff rooms reading the *Times Educational Supplement* flamboyantly for information about the latest research findings in education, defiantly when looking for new teaching posts, and surreptitiously when surveying the advertisements for professional development courses. Attendance on such courses was regarded as a private activity and a means of temporary escape from the classroom. Even when schools or local education authorities paid the fees, there was rarely a forum for reporting back about the learning on the course. Hence changes suggested by attendance on courses were not acceptable to other members of staff. The only benefit could be to the individual teachers attending the course, as professional development and more material for curriculae vitae. Much of the learning within the Kolb cycle could not continue since the course ran in a vacuum, well away from the work in school.

There is still a place for attendance on development programmes away from school, especially for more senior managers who benefit from time to reflect, time to work out difficulties within their teams, and an opportunity to meet other teachers with the same problems. However, for these programmes to be most effective, they must be anchored into the reality of the work back in school, and they must offer an opportunity to plan acceptable changes back at school. Such programmes must no longer be isolated but should be planned within the needs of the whole school.

The local management of schools, in giving schools more financial responsibility for their activities, has enabled schools to plan more carefully for their staff development. And in doing so, participants on such programmes as ours have a forum for planning change back at school. Many of our participants have negotiated specific changes to be planned after, or as a result of attendance on our programmes. Some part of the last day of each of our modules is spent either in making action plans about going back into school, or in using the resources of the literature, the library and each other to begin to plan major changes at school. The literature describing our programmes warns that:

> There will be an opportunity to plan 'real' changes based on the needs of members' institutions. These plans can be used back at participants' places of work.

Our participants come with relevant material to make the plans. After we have offered opportunities for concrete experiences, reflective observation, and abstract conceptualisation, the planning, or active experimentation part of the cycle helps to make sense of the learning experiences, and also to root them into the reality of the workplace.

We have found that time for active experimentation should be carefully planned so that participants are able to make most use of the resources offered to them. So we suggest that they work in pairs to frame their area of planning, asking each other questions based on the learning from the programme. We also ask them to display their areas of exploration so that all the participants can see each others' work — this is as an encouragement to use each other as part of the resources offered. Then we give them enough time to become involved in the planning. It is at this point that most participants decide that they would like to begin to write about their plans as part of the accreditation for the programme. Although the writing is optional, participants have come to value writing as a means of reflecting on their work, and ask for tutoring at this point.

So, the report of the School Management Task Force has served both to remind us to link the learning on the programme to the work back in schools, and to enable time for real and useful planning for that work, within the programmes.

Developing courses for women in educational management

As a result of the visit from the Senior Inspector in a local education authority mentioned at the beginning of this chapter, we realised that we would like to try to address the specific difficulties women thought they might encounter as senior managers in education. We discussed whether to offer courses specifically for women, or whether to place our thinking about women as managers more centrally in *all* our management development programmes. After all, the women we want to encourage into educational management work with men and boys.

We were interested in the research described by Marilyn Davidson and Cary Cooper (1992):

> Authors argue strongly that research evidence has proved that all-women management groups are less threatening and enable women not to be dominated by the dominant group (men!) in terms of speech, role allocation, loyalty affiliation, risk-taking and needs identifications. Certainly, in relation to the acquisition of managerial skills, confidence building and assertiveness training, there is evidence that many all-women courses have proved to be successful. (p.51)

We decided to experiment by offering a three day introduction to management course for women only, but we also wanted to embed notions of gender in management and management styles into all our programmes.

We approached the Centre for Research in Education and Gender (CREG), and a group of seven women, based both at the Institute of Education and 'in the field' set up a course team. We decided to develop the three day course as 'Women into Management', and we ran it for the first time in Summer 1991, with nearly twenty participants, including most of the planning team. The course team were so excited by the course we were planning that we decided to take part in it when we were not facilitating it. The collaborative nature of the course was reinforced by our participation, and seemed enhanced by the presence of the whole team.

As might be expected, the programme was an amalgamation of the developmental working methods of the MDC, the framework of feminist research findings from CREG, and suggestions for successful personal strategies from a woman headteacher. It was successful, and had an air of co-operation and exploration about it that we did not recognise from the courses we run for women and men together. Even when we subsequently ran the course with only two tutors, it was more collaborative than our other programmes. Many of the activities were the ones we use in our usual Management Development Centre programmes, but the outcomes were often very different. For example, diagrammatically and in small groups, we explore participants' organisations, their positions within the structure, and the official and unofficial power bases and decision-making routes. In the ensuing discussion, the course facilitator draws out notions of micropolitics that a manager has to be aware of. In the Women into Management course, the discussion turned to issues of equal opportunities because of the difficulties women and some people from ethnic minorities might have in gaining access to the unofficial power bases, if for example, they meet in the pub after school, or if they are built around a staff football team. This led on to discussions of ethics — having recognised and understood the 'other' decision-making routes, should they be opened up? Infiltrated? Ignored? What does a manager with integrity do?

Subsequently, this particular programme, unlike most of our 'generic' management programmes, has not always recruited enough participants to run regularly. We wonder whether this may have something to do with the cost of supply cover and the place of women-only courses in school time. Sheelagh Harris (1992) recognises this difficulty:

> In the struggle to make the most effective use of scarce resources, management and career development may seem a costly indulgence. Try explaining to the governing body why one member of staff should attend an expensive preparation for headship course or a female teacher go on a 'Women as Managers' course. (p. 30)

However, members of the same planning team have developed a Women as Teachers and Managers module for the Womens' Studies MA and for the MA in Educational Management and Administration, and we are incorporating much of our learning from the Women into Management course into the generic management courses we run at the Management Development Centre.

Evaluating the learning on our programmes

As in the 'active experimentation' phase of the Kolb cycle, we place great importance on the evaluation of our programmes, both as a course team, and with our participants. We work very closely, incorporating suggestions for change into subsequent programmes. We always begin planning new programmes by reading the evaluations from previous ones. There are difficulties, however, with the evaluation of learning when it is based upon Kolb's cycle. As Schön (1990) writes:

> It is always difficult to say what a student has finally learned from the experience of a reflective [programme]. It is especially difficult to say with reasonable certainty what she has *not* learned, for the experience of the [programme] can take root in the subsoil of the mind, in Dewey's phrase, assuming ever-new meanings in the course of a person's further development. And background learning absorbed in a [programme] may become evident only when a student enters a new context where she sees what she has learned as she detects how different she is from those around her.
>
> More immediate judgements about what has been learned are bound to be partial and proximate. Nevertheless, it is possible to describe some of the dimensions of learning outcomes . . . (p.168)

We have always embedded evaluation in our programmes, partly as a form of reflection on learning for the participants, and partly for us to attempt to judge the effectiveness of our work. So we always ask people to answer some very open-ended questions at the end of the programme. However, the difficulty alluded to by Schön soon becomes apparent — we do not want people to try to explain all their learning immediately after a programme. We want to make some space for the 'ever-new meanings' to become clear during the concrete experiences back at the work place. But we still want to know whether our work has been effective. So we have devised a questionnaire to send to participants of the courses that last at least nine days and are based upon a cyclical pattern. We send them six months after the end of our programmes, to see whether we have offered participants a useful learning experience, and also whether their roles have changed since (and possibly as a result of) our work together.

The arrival of the second batch of returning six month follow-up questionnaires prompted a development in our research programme. We looked very carefully at the questionnaires — was there a difference in the responses from men and women? Was there a difference in access to courses and promotion, was there a difference in concepts of management? Was there a difference in learning styles? As the questionnaires came back to us we realised that we were right at the beginning of our research. So with more clearly framed areas of exploration, we developed an interview schedule to explore the area in more detail. The results are reported in Chapter 8.

References

Agnew, D. (1989) 'A world of women' in De Lyon, H. and Widdowson Migniuolo, F. (eds) *Women Teachers — Issues and Experiences* Milton Keynes: Open University Press.

Al-Khalifa, E. (1989) 'Management by halves: women teachers and school managers' in De Lyon H. and Widdowson Migniuolo, F. (eds) *Women*

Teachers — Issues and Experiences Milton Keynes: Open University Press.

Belbin, M. (1981) *Management Teams, Why They Succeed or Fail* Oxford: Heinemann.

Boud, D. and Feletti, G. (eds) (1991) *The Challenge of Problem Based Learning* London: Kogan Page.

Brookfield, S. D. (1986) *Understanding and Facilitating Adult Learning* Milton Keynes: Open University Press.

Burnard, P. (1989) *Teaching Interpersonal Skills: A handbook of experiential learning for health professionals* London: Chapman and Hall.

Davidson, M. and Cooper C. (1992) *Shattering the Glass Ceiling* London: Paul Chapman.

Harris, S. (1992) 'The shifting focus of teacher development: the impact of current trends on the provision of management development for teachers' *Teacher Development* **1**, 1, February.

Jaques, D. (1991) *Learning in Groups* London: Kogan Page.

Kolb, D. A. (1984) *Experiential Learning* New Jersey: Prentice-Hall.

Marshall, C. (1992) *The Assistant Principal, Leadership Choices and Challenges* California: Corwin Press.

Ouston, J., Gold, A. and Gosling, P. (1992) The Development of Managers in Education. Paper given at the BEMAS Research Conference, Nottingham, Easter.

Schön, D. A. (1987) *Educating the Reflective Practitioner: Towards a New Design for Teaching and Learning in the Professions* San Francisco: Jossey Rass.

Schön, D. A. (1990) *Educating the Reflective Practitioner* San Francisco: Jossey-Bass.

School Management Task Force (1990) *Developing School Management — The Way Forward* HMSO.

Warner Weil, S. and McGill, I. (eds.) (1989) *Making Sense of Experiential Learning* Milton Keynes: SRHE and Open University Press.

7 Women and management training in the 1990s

Hilary Atchison

This chapter reflects on the provision of management training for women teachers in the 1990s. Discussion will focus on issues related to training for senior management rather than professional development, i.e. women managers rather than women *into* management. It will also demonstrate how my own learning has influenced my practice in relation to my role as an advisory teacher for gender equality with responsibility for training/providing INSET for women teachers. The chapter begins by discussing the current issues for management training in the national and local contexts and considering the particular position of women. I then examine the factors influencing the design, content and running of the course I developed with reference to the MDC course I attended. I end by drawing some tentative conclusions about management training for women in the future based on the course participants' evaluations, my evaluation and reflections on the course.

The context for training in the 1990s

In setting up training courses and assessing training needs for school management there are a number of issues to be taken into consideration concerning the national and local education contexts in which schools/school managers operate. In making a training needs assessment for courses traditionally there has been no differentiation identifed between male and female participants in relation to school management. It has been seen as a neutral activity — or a non-issue. In other words it has been gender blind. On most courses currently on offer and in most of the school management literature women are invisible or marginalised, with a few notable exceptions, e.g. Ball (1987). This is hardly surprising given that educational culture, headship and leadership have always been seen as male concepts (Al-Khalifa 1989):

> . . . the organisation of primary schooling suggests that there are clearly defined roles for male and female teachers, equating the classroom with domesticity and school management with leadership and power which have traditionally had a male connotation. (Burgess 1989, p. 81)

However the current intensification of 'management' has exacerbated the situation to the extent that we have to talk about 'women *into* management' and for many women that is still an anathema. Courses are male dominated in terms of the number of participants, the content and process of the course and the associated reading texts (mostly written by men). It is assumed either that the 'manager' is a man or if in rare instances, a woman, that there is no difference — it is unisex. The particular experience and contribution of women is ignored. But being a woman manager does raise different issues from that of men and for black women managers the issues are different again (Al-Khalifa 1989). In the case of women managers in the 1990s therefore, the issue is whether their needs can be met by providing mixed courses or whether specific women only courses are the solution.

National context

The current focus on school management has taken on a new importance and urgency since the ERA, the National Curriculum, the introduction of LMS, open enrolment and teacher appraisal but in itself it dates back some years to the movement for 'effective schools' following studies such as the Rutter report 1979 and the literature on 'excellence' (Peters and Waterman 1982, Peters 1988). However, for many years it was argued that schools were very different from other types of organisation with the effect that they did not keep up to date with current management theory and practice which has now moved on well beyond the simplistic functional organisational model with its associations of both organisational leaders with masculinity and leadership with hierarchy (Handy 1989). As a result heads and deputies were either more concerned with administration rather than management or into 'gee whizzery' heroic styles of management and leadership and certainly did not view themselves as part of a genuine team. Functional roles and responsibilities were sharply divided into the curriculum deputy — invariably male — and the pastoral deputy — invariably female. But the political, social and economic context in which schools are operating has changed dramatically during the last six years and there has been radical reform of the education system. It is now firmly established that schools need to have a coherent management approach particularly in relation to the management of change, institutional development planning and the management of resources human and otherwise (Beare *et al.* 1989, Davies *et al.* 1990). New skills and competences are required in senior managers as schools face up to a period of increasing challenge and change but many are stuck in traditional models of organisation and modes of operating (Jenkins 1991). There is therefore a great need for training if schools and teachers are to be able to cope with increasing demands. Peters (1988) suggests that quality is really about training and unlocking the potential of the workforce, which can only be done by moving away from hierarchy to the position where everyone is a manager — 'the front line people'. What is being suggested is a reconceptualisation of management and leadership (Handy 1989, Peters 1989). A feminist perspective might therefore be more appropriate and have much to offer to today's modern management (Blackmore 1989, Fritchie 1989). Focusing on women's concerns and women's role in management highlights the inadequacies of the present concept (Al-Khalifa 1989). Moreover as Al-Khalifa suggests:

> knowledge and experience of gender-linked issues are not normally required preparation for management, and demonstrable skills in relating to women staff and girl pupils are not sought out as necessary for the performance of staff and pupil management. It is one of the anomalies of the literature on management and its practice, that headteachers can be considered 'effective' while disregarding the needs of girl pupils and demonstrating ineptitude in their relationship with women colleagues.

As a provider then there is a challenge as to how best to deliver training to meet these new needs.

Local context

As schools have had to face the challenge of the educational revolution, so have LEAs. The major issue concerning provision of training is over changes in funding from GEST and greater devolution of the schools budget to schools. At a time when more training is required LEAs have less money available centrally. So the concern centres around the most cost-effective way to provide quality training which is appropriate. Hounslow LEA has opted to run in-house courses as opposed to funding individuals to study elsewhere. A mixed course for middle managers has run several times as a long twilight course and after a long hard struggle by women in the borough, a professional development foundation course for women has been prioritised as the main long course funded from this budget. In addition a three day short course for Women in Management (WIM) for middle managers has been prioritised and funded from the gender equality budget for reasons which shall be explained in the following section.

Women as teachers and managers

Whilst this decade has been promoted as Opportunity 2000 — a new era of opportunity for women in employment and for women as leaders and managers, women in teaching seem to be losing out rather than gaining (Al-Khalifa 1989). Although teaching has become a 'feminised' profession attracting fewer male recruits, with women comprising 61 per cent of the total workforce and 80 per cent of primary teachers, it is still the case that women are located in the lower levels, on main scale and in supply teaching whereas men have an increased chance of gaining allowances and head or deputy headships (De Lyon and Widdowson-Migniuolo 1989). At primary level men comprise 20 per cent of the teaching force but hold 53 per cent of headteachers posts and 39 per cent deputies posts. In the secondary sector women form 45 per cent of the workforce but only 3 per cent of women in contrast to 8 per cent of men are headteachers or deputies (1987 NUT survey). Men in secondary schools are three times more likely than women to gain D or E allowances (DES statistics 1989). Out of 26,000 women part-timers few receive any incentive allowance while 300 of the 3,600 male part-timers get a D or E allowance (Secondary Staffing survey 1988). From the limited data available (CRE survey 1988) we know that ethnic minority women are even more under-represented in senior posts. Furthermore, there is a sharp distinction between the kind of posts held by men and women which further marginalises women in terms of future career prospects and promotion:

> If we consider the modal location of men and women teachers, we observe that men and women typically teach different subjects to different groups of children, and generally have different chances for rewards within the system. (Acker 1983, p.123)

Women are expected to do more or different kinds of things to gain promotion (UMIST survey and MOSS surveys quoted in Doe 1989). The recent AMMA secondary survey also shows that women are teaching larger classes on lower salaries. Women were heads of year or heads of lower and upper school, or heads of special education, cross school liaison jobs. Men were heads of faculty or sixth form which are straightforward visible management jobs which lead directly to promotion as deputy heads (Doe 1989). This mirrors the situation in general in business organisations (Fritchie 1989).

There are many factors which affect women's opportunities and career development including women's own understanding about their development and career needs and a belief that there is greater satisfaction to be gained from class teaching. However it is not intended to discuss the complexities of these issues in this chapter as they are more relevant to professional and management development in general. As far as women managers for the course under discussion are concerned, they were already committed to considering going for promotion.

It appears that far more important factors operating at this level are the many myths and stereotyped assumptions used by headteachers and other (male) teachers to explain why this situation exists. They suggest that women are underqualified, not interested in furthering their careers, do not apply for top jobs, have children and therefore do not seek promotion, take career breaks and therefore lose impetus for a career, will not move house to pursue promotion, are unwilling to undertake INSET, and have different reasons for seeking promotion. However recent studies of women's location in the system in relation to careers indicates a very different picture showing systematic patterns of discrimination (Evetts 1990, Doe 1989, Al-Khalifa 1989, NUT 1987, ILEA, Warwickshire 1989, Birmingham surveys). In relation to training, surveys show that women and men have fairly equal levels of INSET participation; the difference lies in the type of courses they pursue. Men predominate on courses connected with management skills and women on curriculum related courses. The surveys also show that women are less likely than men to be released from school for INSET than men (ILEA, Warwickshire 1989 and Birmingham surveys). Hence male managers act as 'gatekeepers' to women's development in terms of perceptions of suitability for promotion and access to training and development (Al-Khalifa 1989, Ball 1987, Grant 1989).

There is therefore a great need for management training for women to make progress within the system, for the system to gain the most from 61 per cent of its workers and for feminist perspectives at management level to change the system itself. Research on American schools (Shakeshaft 1987) suggests that:

> where women fill senior management positions the achievement level in reading and maths is higher and there is less violence and student and staff morale is high.

Women can bring a different perspective and ways of working which would benefit the education system as a whole.

Women themselves are demanding access to management training and raising issues through their unions (NUT conference 1992). Many women see this as an individual enterprise in gaining access to power and status as an equal rights issue. However when in positions of power, as many female primary headteachers today, they do not see the need for supporting and encouraging other women teachers but take the attitude 'I made it, why can't she?' (Ball 1987). But on the other hand there are many other feminist women, myself included, who want to progress to positions of power in order to influence and change the system itself. In gaining power we do not want to have to behave like a man, i.e. the Margaret Thatcher syndrome; we want something qualitatively different:

> We want a change in school management — feminine characteristics are currently devalued, we want account to be taken of qualities which women particularly can bring to school management and ways of working which women appear to value and prefer, but which differ from the norms and values of school management generally (quote from women heads and deputies in Al-Khalifa 1989).

There is therefore a need for providing a qualitatively different course for women as women managers offering a transformational model of management in order to change the system, empower and bring on other women through the system, ensure delivery of equal opportunities in education and improve the education of girls. The challenge is can such a course also attract those career-oriented non-feminist women and challenge their atitiudes, change perspectives and radicalise them in the so called 'post feminist era' to gain and mobilise support rather than just meet the needs of the converted. A further issue is can women obtain release from school to attend such courses. In addition there is also a strong case to be made for management courses which challenge male managers' misconceptions about women teachers/managers and challenge the outmoded 'male' model of management itself and develop understanding of the gender dynamics in the workplace, issues for women at work and girls in school.

In Hounslow the need for quality management training in the LEA in the current context has been established. There is a commitment to positive action for training for women because of their location in the system. From experience in running the Women's Professional Development Course it is recognised that women are not a homogenous group and it is necessary to provide for differentiation and progression for women teachers. It was therefore decided to provide a new short course for Women in Management (WIM) to try to attract a variety of women middle managers to achieve those aims outlined above. A women only course was considered necessary and by offering a high quality management course it was hoped to attract participants from both feminist and non-feminist, black and working class women. So such a course could be part of a coherent programme of courses and meet these different sets of needs.

Issues in course design

Having clarified the context within which training is provided, issues in the course design, content and delivery will be discussed. Many INSET programmes including those provided in Hounslow LEA adopt a top down transmission model similar to that illustrated in Figure 7.1 (Mumford 1986).

professional development designed by 'experts'

↓

knowledge presented as universal in application

↓

transfer to own situation

↓

difficulty in application

↓

minimal impact

Figure 7.1

Such a model cannot work in relation to training adults nor is it a suitable model to offer in education. From personal experience in attending other courses this model does little to facilitate learning or to change practice. It is the process involved in training which is of paramount importance in relation to successful learning outcomes and must be built in to the course at the design stage. The MDC course was an excellent example reflecting the importance given to the nature and status of the adult learner and to the identification of appropriate strategies for learning. It reinforced previous personal learning about training and is very similar to the type of training enabling strategies and possibilities for change.

Knowles (1984) argues that in adult learning (andragogy as opposed to pedagogy) a learner has the following characteristics:

- s/he is largely self-directed and requires a climate of trust, collaboration and openness to learn effectively;
- the previous experience of the learner has to be implicit in the learning process, it is too substantial and significant to the individual to be ignored;
- the adult learner has to accept the need to learn, i.e. it must be perceived as being of personal value;

- s/he is biased towards problem-solving as a learning activity;
- practical relevance will be a significant factor in obtaining commitment;
- s/he will only internalise learning if motivated by intrinsic factors.

If this is accepted then it has obvious implications for the role of the trainer and the training methods employed. It follows that the most appropriate model of learning is active or 'experiential learning' (Kolb 1984) which will empower teachers (see Figure 7.2).

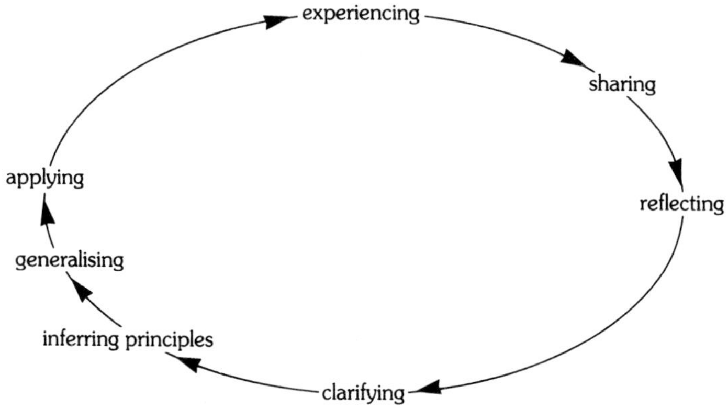

Figure 7.2 – The Kolb learning cycle

This was modelled on the MDC course. It is a very effective model as learning on the course has clearly influenced personal practice as a manager in terms of personal management skills and other aspects of the job and also as a trainer. The training philosophy which underpins the WIM course is based therefore on the same values expressed by Knowles and Kolb relating to adult learning. It is considered that INSET should:

- be active/participatory: the facilitator is not an expert but someone enabling supportive group work and is concerned with process as much as task;
- recognise that all people have equal worth and need to feel valued; positive learning takes place when the learner feels valued;
- acknowledge that learning takes place when support and encouragement are offered in an atmosphere of trust, i.e. when participants feel able to try out new ideas without being judged;
- build from the learner's own experiences;

- develop understanding by providing the opportunity for participants to think through the issues, explore different viewponts and reflect on their own experiences and practice;
- acknowledge that there are no clear cut answers and there is a need for creative work which relates the issues to the particular school situation;
- encourage the learner to take responsibility for her own learning;
- empower not deskill; it should develop the skills and provide the support to translate understanding into practical strategies and action.

Course design therefore should begin from a needs analysis, taking account of the needs of the task, the participants and the trainer/facilitator. Only then can appropriate learning activities be planned. In the case of the WIM course participants were given the opportunity to identify their own needs at the initial stage on their application forms and these were taken into account in the planning. The needs were seen as shown in Figure 7.3 below.

These sets of needs have similarities with the MDC course but are also different in relation to the particular needs of women managers and the trainer's own particular view of the task in hand as already expressed in the previous section. Therefore it was possible to devise a course which drew much from the learning and experiences on the MDC course but also needed to incorporate additional aspects relating to women within the limitations imposed by a three day course as opposed to the nine days of the MDC course.

In terms of pacing, the balance of activities between input, small group work, whole group, role play etc. was very similar but of necessity the WIM course was probably more intensive. The other issue of pacing which was found to be very valuable on the MDC course was the gap between modules to allow time for reflection, assimilation and practical experimentation. Although the WIM course was only three days, it was therefore decided to run two days, an intervening gap of two weeks, followed by the third day. Thus the course devised is intensive, skill focused, and practice based, focused on being a manager. For women this means taking yourself seriously, taking the job seriously, going for promotion and supporting other women. To support this it was also decided to run the course at the Hounslow Business Centre which is part of the Hounslow Borough College as it was considered to be a 'non-teachery' environment with concern for quality and more appropriate to the culture which it was hoped to create on the course. This proved to be a significant success factor.

Figure 7.3 – Course design needs analysis

current education management context

skills and knowledge to be an effective manager

pacing and balance

context for women teachers

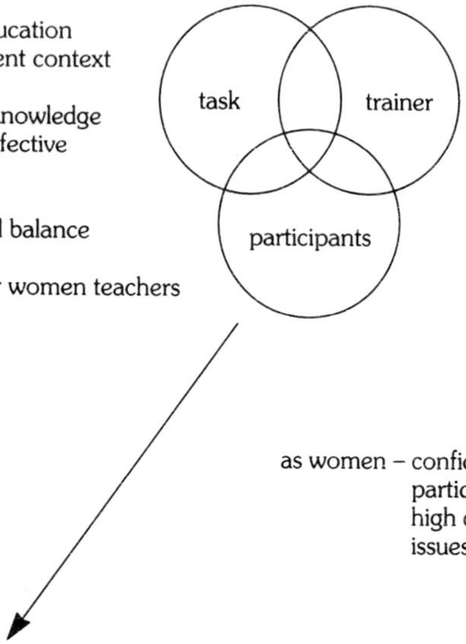

personal philosophy
adult learning

empower women

focus on process

develop support networks

as women – confidence building
particular skills
high quality course
issues as women managers

broad aims and goals
to enable participants to:

- develop a personal vision of education and leadership;
- recognise and build on strengths, manage and improve areas of weakness and enhance individual effectiveness in the workplace;
- develop a range of practical management skills and build confidence;
- provide a forum for women managers to explore their role.

Issues of content

Whilst acknowledging that process and content are difficult to separate, this section will attempt to focus specifically on content, making the links between learning on the MDC course and teaching/ training as an advisory teacher.

Broadly speaking the aims and objectives of both courses were not dissimilar. This is perhaps not surprising given the same educational philosophy and similar context for the training. There were differences however given the particular needs of women which the WIM course was trying to meet. With any course there are time constraints and decisions have to be made about what content is appropriate and how much can be delivered in the time. There was nothing on the MDC which was considered to be irrelevant or not valuable but certain missing areas were identified. Therefore ruthless decisions had to be taken. The two main areas which had to be excluded were the management of change and staff development — module 3. It was felt that the management of change was being covered in the borough on several other courses, e.g. Women's Professional Development Foundation Course, Gender Co-ordinators Courses and the Multicultural Course and this should be fed back into schools. Likewise all teachers in the borough have had appraisal and staff development training and although this has not highlighted gender issues, could not be given priority. The major problem was therefore that of trying to extract and condense from the remaining two modules and add in new sections.

Creating the right kind of climate/culture at the beginning was considered of primary importance to the success of the course even though there was a premium on time. From the MDC course it was recognised that this would be time well spent. A supportive, friendly, relaxed yet purposeful atmosphere where people felt they could open to themselves and each other was successfully established through the *introductions, agreeing some groundrules and the icebreaker activity*. This revealed a range of women's experiences and a number of patterns emerged which were common to many of the group. In addition it highlighted the role that significant others had played in helping and supporting people's development. This was an important learning point for all in thinking about their vision and their own roles and responsibilities as women managers. The *Women in Britain Quiz* gave a context for individual experiences, highlighted significant patterns and proved an effective tool in raising awareness.

The session *Being a Senior Manager* was based almost entirely on the activities from the MDC course, drawing on participants' own knowledge and ideas. The difference on the WIM course was that the women did raise the issue of which of those might be considered traditionally male/female qualities and which skills might come more easily to women or men. Many issues were raised and participants were able to challenge each other. This was then put in the context of modern management skills and the sort of roles and positions which women occupy and the implications of this for careers.

As the *SWOT analysis method* was found to be very useful on the MDC course, it was applied to the WIM course for participants to undertake a *personal skills audit* in relation to being an effective manager. *Working through teams* and *You as a team person* were also highly effective on the MDC course but the teambuilding activity had to be excluded due to time. It was replaced by the Video Arts programme based on Belbin from which ideas were drawn in relation to choosing a team and job specs, relating it to current work teams. *Leadership styles* built on the individual exercise from the MDC course and took it beyond to consider *male/female styles*, moving on to *transformational leadership and situational leadership* in relation to the context/structure of the organisation and time scale to which one is working. Although this was developed as a result of further reading it was felt that the MDC course was suggesting ideas along similar lines.

The second day focused on *personal management skills and managing people.* Again due to time constraints it was not possible to do a full session on time management however that is covered on the previously mentioned foundation course. An *'in-tray' exercise* was devised as an alternative which was then linked to defining criteria for effectiveness in the job. This led into a *structured exercise on delegation* taken from the MDC course. The MDC session on assertiveness was one of the least valuable parts of the course from a personal point of view. Having personally run a considerable amount of assertiveness training, the issues in trying to get people to be confident in role play and open up and the need for actually teaching the basic skills of assertiveness are well understood. Consequently it was found to be far too superficial and was not really effective for the group. Therefore, for the WIM course it was decided to exclude it, particularly as assertiveness is run as a separate short course in the LEA. One of the critical issues, particularly for women is *managing non-performance.* So a session was devised which also included *assertive communication.* The feedback was that this session was one of the most useful parts of the course but needed more time, indicating again the difficulties of getting people into any kind of role play on a two day module.

Running effective meetings was a slightly adapted version of the MDC course and again participants found it extremely valuable. The session *Being a woman manager* gave the opportunity for participants to consider issues at work, being a role model, empowering other women and projecting confidence. This was a crucial session which drew upon the rest of the course, pulled much of it together and put it into the context of the reality for women managers. The question is should and could it be made more of an issue on mixed courses also.

Reflections

In this section the possible implications of these experiences for the provision of management training for women in the future will be considered. Are women only courses the solution?

From the WIM course evaluations and personal observations it seems that women only courses are certainly necessary in terms of providing a safe arena for women to talk *qua* women about the issues including harassment. This certainly did not happen on the MDC course although attempts were made to draw in issues for women at appropriate moments. Despite the excellent supportive learning environment which had been created on the course I did not feel able to raise many of the issues which I would have liked as it did not seem legitimate to do so. It should not be up to the participants to have to take this on. There is a feeling of 'oh not again'. Often when one does speak up one feels like an alien from another planet. Making an explicit slot on the programme for this gives it status and legitimacy. Perhaps a discussion time for a separate men's and women's group which could have come together later may have solved this. However there is always the issue that it is seen as irrelevant by the men and for many women also it is a non-issue.

The all female WIM course also had a very different 'feel' to it. There was no time wasted on unnecessary issues and having to listen to men talking about irrelevancies; no time wasted having to challenge men's attitudes and sexist behaviour which came as welcome relief. It was very focused, task oriented and extremely hard working. Even at the end of the first day there was a tremendously stimulating and empowering feel to it. Women felt encouraged to be confident about the validity of their own experience and ideas about their own needs and approaches to management. As Debra wrote in her evaluation:

> I recognised good practice in myself and felt good. It helped me identify areas that I could work on and improve. It crystallised ideas that I have and gave me confidence to carry on with the way I was doing things.

Women felt so good about it and were so appreciative of something special of high quality for them. They felt that, as teachers, they were treated like adults for the first time. At the beginning of the third day, the centre manager had accidentally written 'Teachers' Course room 2' on the notice board. There was a huge protest from the women saying 'we're not teachers, we're managers!' They were obviously feeling very different about themselves and much more positive and comfortable about the whole concept of management and how it can be transformed. This was also borne out and reported in Al-Khalifa (1989). Sue wrote in her evaluation:

> I feel that the 'mystery' of being a manager has been removed. I feel that I have learnt what it is about me that I can develop as a manager and I have also gained some very practical ideas and strategies to use myself and share with colleagues.

There had also been a turnaround or radicalisation for many of the women in terms of relating to other women and their future role as headteachers in encouraging other women with positive action.

Questions were also asked and demands made about similar courses for their own headteachers. The women felt there was a great need for this in the LEA. However that is another issue, as headteachers' training is not within my remit. Such courses, then, do have the potential to radicalise women managers who may not previously have had the opportunity to even consider the issues, learn of other research and put their individual experiences into a context.

Did it provide the kind of knowledge and skills to equip them to compete with men for management positions? It certainly built confidence in their abilities to take on leadership roles and 'go for it' and clarified their thinking of why they wanted promotion in terms of developing and implementing their vision 'making it happen'. All women mentioned the confidence building, the validation and the courage to pursue their own vision and goals as major gains from the course. Building confidence certainly is very important but not sufficient. There has to be a sound foundation of knowledge and skills. It did provide the basis for going on to further development in practice for most of the personal management and people management skills required. What was missing were the management of resources and curriculum skills but these were also absent from the MDC course. On a short course one has to prioritise and there are many other courses for these aspects. Furthermore once women have been given the opportunity to identify their needs, as they were able to do on the WIM course, they can and should take responsibility for their own further learning. A spontaneous support group and networking have also been outcomes of the course. This group now meets regularly twice a term and has identified a programme of further training which they are going to develop as well as supporting each other.

Thus I would suggest that such courses are necessary for women but not sufficient for changing the system at a structural/deeper level. The question of whether women can be released from their schools to attend such courses remains a difficult one. The WIM course was heavily oversubscribed but the vast majority of applications were from primary teachers. This indicates that it did not seem to be a problem for them to come on a women's course, particularly if their head was female even though not necessarily a feminist. Whereas at secondary level only a few applications were received. Subsequently some enquiries were made of women secondary teachers who attended the alternative course for middle managers which was run as a long twilight mixed course by a man, who is a well known deputy head in the LEA. Many of these women said they had been 'advised' by their male heads that this would be 'better' for their career development and they could not obtain daytime release for the other course despite it being fully funded.

There need to be changes in the type of management courses currently run for mixed groups which tend to be male dominated as described earlier. I have recently attended a management course run by a woman who paid lip service to gender issues and used a male transmission model of training. I also attended a course run by a man who used a process model of training but had absolutely no awareness of gender issues in the content of the course or gender dynamics in the interactions between participants and displayed a patronising attitude to female participants. There was almost a walk-out by the women!

The MDC course went a long way towards achieving a new model. It was interesting that there was a good balance between male/female participants and that the course was run by women who were aware of gender issues/implications and who were committed to a process model of training and a transformational model of management. But still I felt that the men were not sufficiently challenged to take on the gender issues. There was far too much complacency and it did not get beyond the individual level to the deeper structural level, i.e. if we behave as model managers, teambuilders etc. — both men and women — there would be no problem. For women on the course too there was no building of solidarity, empowerment and commitment to positive action for other women. It is understood that this was not part of the aims of the course but I would argue that there is a need for it if real change is going to come about.

What both courses have revealed, therefore, in terms of management training for women, is the need for both kinds of courses. Courses for women only are vital but not sufficient. Unfortunately some women's courses are too 'soft and fluffy' and unfocused, just a talking shop. Such courses need to be of the highest quality possible to offer real opportunity for development of knowledge and skills and recognise strengths in management. On the other hand mixed courses which do not address the real issues of male domination of management, challenge the male concept of management and take a critical approach to reading texts and issues for women managers simply remain at the level of rhetoric, appropriate the language of collaborative participation and maintain the status quo. Men need to hear what women have to say. There needs to be change on all education management courses in terms of content, process and gender awareness of facilitators. Failure to do so will result in the needs of 60 per cent of the teaching force being unmet, failure to utilise the skills and experience which women have to offer and failure to offer an education service to all (Al-Khalifa 1989). I believe the MDC course offers a suitable model for such a new course but needs to incorporate the above mentioned issues more explicitly. Furthermore, there should continue to be courses for women only to build the necessary confidence, to radicalise women and improve the education of girls until such time as we live in an ungendered society. Whether they will be 'allowed' to happen and whether women will be 'allowed' to attend them is an interesting question.

References

Acker, S. (1983) 'Women and teaching: a semi-detached sociology of a semi-profession' in Walker, S. and Barton, L. (eds) *op cit.*

Acker, S. (1989) *Teachers Gender and Careers* London: Falmer.

Agnew, D. (1989) 'A world of women: an approach to personal and career development for women teachers in primary schools' in De Lyon, H. and Widdowson-Magniuolo, F. (eds) *op cit.*

Al-Khalifa, E. (1989) 'Management by halves: women teachers and school management' in De Lyon, H. and Widdowson-Magniuolo, F. (eds) *op cit.*

Ball, S. J. (1987) *The Micro-politics of the School: Towards a Theory of School Organisation*, London: Routledge.

Beare *et al.* (1989) *Creating an Excellent School* London: Routledge.

Blackmore, J. (1989) 'Educational Leadership a feminist critique and reconstruction' in Smyth, J. (ed.) *op cit.*

Burgess, H. (1989) 'A sort of career: women in primary schools' in Skelton, C. (ed.) *op cit.*

Clarke, D. and Coleman, G (1990) *Management Effectiveness for Women* NEC.

Davies, B. *et al.* (eds) (1990) *Education Management for the 1990s* Harlow: Longman.

De Lyon, H. and Widdowson-Magniuolo, F. (eds) (1989) *Women Teachers: Issues and Experiences* Milton Keynes: Open University Press.

Doe, B. (1989) 'Heads, he wins and she loses' *Times Education Supplement* 27 October.

Evetts, J. (1989) *Women in Primary Teaching: Career Contexts and Strategies* London: Unwin Hyman.

Fritchie, F. (1989) 'Process Mary, task Harry' *Women and Training News* 28.

Grant, R. (1989) 'Women teachers career pathways: towards an alternative model of career' in Acker, S. (ed.) *op cit.*

Handy, C. (1989) *The Age of Unreason* Business Books Ltd.

Jenkins, H.O. (1991) *Getting it Right: A Handbook of Successful School Leadership* Oxford: Blackwell

Kolb, D.A. (1984) *Experiential Learning: Experience as a Source of Learning and Development* Englewood Cliffs. Prentice Hall.

Knowles, M.S. (1984) *Andragogy in Action* London: McGraw Hill.

Mumford, A. (1986) *Handbook of Management Development*, Gower

Peters, T. (1988) *Thriving on Chaos* London: Macmillan.

Peters, T. and Waterman, R. (1982) *In Search of Excellence* London: Macmillan.

Ranger, C. (1988) *Ethnic Minority School Teachers*, CRE.

Rutter, T. *et al.* (1979) *15000 hours*

Shakeshaft, C. (1987) *Women in Educational Administration* Sage.

Skelton, C. (ed.) (1989) *Whatever Happens to Little Women?* Falmer.
Smyth, J. (ed.) (1989) *Critical Perspectives on Educational Leadership* London: Falmer
Walker, S. and Barton, L. (eds) (1983) *Gender, Class and Education* London: Falmer.
Warwickshire County Council (1989) *Women Secondary Teachers: A Wasted Resource* Warwick: WCC.

8 The development of managers in education

Janet Ouston, Anne Gold and Peggy Gosling

Introduction

This chapter is a report of work in progress. The small scale investigation described here explores the knowledge, skills and qualities that education managers need to learn to carry out their roles effectively and how they acquire them.

The study grew out of the work of the Management Development Centre (MDC), which has in recent years developed a focus on the development of interpersonal skills. Managing the people within an organisation is of central importance, and is possibly the most difficult to get right. There are, of course, many other important skills, but poor management of the 'people resource' can undermine performance in other areas such as managing the curriculum or finance. Management is seen as being widely spread across the institution and not merely the task of the headteacher or the senior management team.

Our approach to management development is based in the adult learning model of Kolb (1984) which stresses the importance of working with existing professional (and managerial) experience. The importance of reflection is stressed, which together with new knowledge and concepts, leads to conceptual understanding. The learner is then encouraged to explore and experiment (through discussion and simulation) which in its turn leads to new experiences. Anne Gold's chapter in this book describes the Centre's approach in more detail.

Over the last two years 65 per cent of the participants on nine and twenty day courses run at the Centre have been women. This is similar to the proportion of women teachers (63 per cent) but far greater than the proportion of women currently in senior posts (DES 1992).

The interview study reported here was influenced by several different factors. The competence approach to management in education (Earley 1991, Ouston 1993) has raised the question of how management skills and knowledge can be described. The School Management South development of the Management Charter Initiative Standards (School Management South 1992) divides the management of schools into managing policy, managing learning, managing people and managing resources. We have used these to classify the key tasks of our interviewees.

Our interest in women as managers in education led us to explore whether they showed any different patterns of professional development. We were able to compare the replies of men and women managers to our interview questions and the way in which they interpret and develop their management role.

Centre programmes are regularly evaluated. Participants are asked to complete an evaluation at the end of each course. They are also asked to evaluate their work with us six months later, reflecting on its value in the light of subsequent experience. The interview study reported here grew from these evaluations, but is not merely an evaluation of our own work.

The Task Force Report (DES 1991) stressed the importance of school-based management development. While we too see this as playing a valuable role in managers' growth, participants in our programmes tell us that the development of interpersonal skills can be assisted by working with others away from their own school. Alexander (1991) argued that school-based development can lead to schools recycling their own bad practice; we too feel that higher education has a role to play in management development provided that the out-of-school work is carefully enmeshed with the teacher's own environment.

The research

Purposes of the interview study

The interview study was planned to explore the following issues:

1. The areas of knowledge, skills and personal qualities managers in education consider are required to carry out the key aspects of their role effectively.
2. The experiences they perceive to have influenced the development of these areas of knowledge, skills and personal qualities.
3. Whether attendance at an MDC course has been one of the influences on these developments.

4. Are there any consistent differences between men and women in their reports of their responsibilities, their perceptions of, and influences on, the knowledge, skills or qualities required for effective education management?
5. This study was planned as a feasibility study for a larger programme of research into the development of education managers. Was the semi-structured interview technique used here acceptable to teachers and did it provide useful information?

These questions will be re-visited towards the end of the chapter.

Participants

All MDC programme participants are sent an evaluation questionnaire six months after the end of the course. The first follow-up mailing, from which the interviewees were taken, had a return rate of 36 per cent. More recently the return rate has risen to over 50 per cent. As part of the follow-up respondents were asked to give a global rating of the contribution of the programme to their development from 1 (very little) to 5 (a major contribution). Of those who returned the questionnaires, 64 per cent gave a rating of 4 or 5. The interviewees are, as a group, more positive; 81.8 per cent gave the course a rating of 4 or 5.

Participants are allowed to return their questionnaires anonymously if they choose, or to sign them. Our interviewees were taken from those who signed their questionnaires. We have, therefore, a group of interviewees who were interested enough in their own management development to return signed questionnaires. For a feasibility study a group of thoughtful, reflective, managers is ideal, but our sample's replies to our interview questions may not reflect those of teachers in general. Of the 26 who gave their names, two could not be contacted and two were unwilling to be interviewed. A total of 22 interviews (11 women and 11 men) were undertaken during February and March 1992.

Background information is shown in Table 8.1. As groups, the men and women were (surprisingly) very similar. Men had, on average, been teachers for slightly longer than the women, and reported taking part in more previous management courses. There were also differences in their qualifications. Ten interviewees (seven men and three men) had taken part in the Centre's Managing SEN (Special Educational Needs) programme, the remainder had taken the primary management programme or the middle and senior management courses that replaced it from 1990–91.

Table 8.1 – Background information about the interviewees

	Women	**Men**	**All**
Age in years			
25–34	2	2	4
35–44	6	6	12
over 45	3	3	6
School type			
Infants	1	0	1
Junior	0	1	1
Primary	2	4	6
Secondary	4	2	6
College	0	1	1
Special	3	3	6
Service	1	0	1
Post			
Head	4	4	8
Deputy	1	2	3
Head of service	1	0	1
HODs	3	3	6
Curriculum co-ordinator	2	2	4
Allowance			
B	3	3	6
C	1	1	2
D	2	0	2
FE (SL)	0	1	1
Deputy Head	1	2	3
Head	4	4	8
Member of the school's senior management team			
No	3	3	6
Yes	8	8	16
Teaching experience			
Average (in years)	16.9	18.6	17.8
Years in post of responsibility			
Average	13.1	14.1	13.6
Qualifications (highest obtained)			
Certificate	0	3	3
BEd	2	0	2
Other first degree	0	3	3
PGCE	0	3	3
Advanced diploma	7	1	8
Masters	2	1	3
Previous management course			
No	9	6	15
Yes—1 or 2	2	5	7

The interviews

The interviews were all undertaken by one person (PG). The interviewer was familiar with the work of the Centre but was not centrally involved in its work. This was made clear to participants.

Potential interviewees were contacted by telephone and the purpose of the study was explained to them. All the participants were asked to complete a pre-interview questionnaire giving details of their post, career history and qualifications. They also all agreed that their interview should be tape-recorded.

Figure 8.1 – Structure of the interview and analysis

In the first stage of the interview, the interviewer introduced herself, the purpose and the format of the interview. A list of four major areas of responsibility were then negotiated. These were based on information given in the questionnaire.

In the third stage of the interview, the interviewer asked a series of open ended questions concerning the essential knowledge, skills and qualities required for effective performance in each of the four areas of responsibility. She asked, for example, 'What is the most important thing you need to know in order to be effective in . . .?'; 'What were the influences on the development of that knowledge?' These questions were repeated for skills and qualities.

For each area of responsibility, the most important area of knowledge, skills and qualities were recorded along with the influences on their development. Some interviewees insisted that two areas were of equal importance, so both were recorded. Up to three influences were recorded for each area of knowledge, skill and quality. In addition, if the interviewee had not said whether the Centre course was an influence on their development they were asked if they had been influenced by any aspect of the course. The structure of the research is shown in Figure 8.1. The figure also shows the categories that were used for summarising the information obtained. These will be discussed in detail later in this paper.

In general, after the structure of the interview was explained, interviewees were able to work through the questions without assistance. Some gave information about why particular areas were important to them, these are summarised later. Many commented that they had enjoyed the interview and the opportunity it gave to reflect on their own development. Each interview took approximately one hour. Five interviewees did not have enough time to complete a full exploration of all four responsibilities.

Results

This is a small scale study, and it will be appreciated that subdividing responses into categories often results in very small numbers within a category. A larger scale study would be able to explore the relationships between responsibilities, knowledge, skills, qualities and influences in greater depth.

The analysis of the interviews is shown in several stages. First, the *responsibilities* reported by the interviewees are summarised, then their perceptions of the *knowledge* required, then the *influences* on knowledge. This approach is repeated for skills and qualities.

Each table shows the number of responses by category. Percentages are sometimes presented to allow comparisons to be made between categories. Percentages are always calculated *down* columns, and comparisons should always be made *across* rows.

Responsibilities

Each of the 22 interviewees gave four main areas of responsibility in their job. These were very diverse: a total of 30 different areas were given. The most frequent was 'the curriculum' (10 people) followed by 'an area of the national curriculum' (8), 'responsible for staff development', 'leading the team' (6), 'organising learning support' (6).

It was clearly necessary to group the replies to explore them in more detail. This was done using the School Management South development of the Management Charter Initiative 'key roles' (Earley 1991). These are managing policy (e.g. contributing to the development of the school development plan), managing learning (e.g. responsibility for an area of the National Curriculum), managing people (e.g. responsibility for staff development) and managing resources (e.g. financial planning). We found it necessary to add two other categories, for administration (e.g. ordering stock and equipment) and the interviewee's own teaching.

Table 8.2 – Responsibilities reported by interviewees

Area of responsibility	Women	Men	All
Policy	3	5	8
Learning	17	16	33
People	15	18	33
Resources	5	2	7
Admin	3	2	5
Own teaching	1	1	2
Total	44	44	88

Table 8.2. shows that the majority of responsibilities reported were coded as managing learning or managing people. Table 8.3 shows that those who were members of the senior management team (SMT) gave many more responsibilities for 'managing people' and this was particularly true for men, as shown in Table 8.4

For each responsibility, interviewees were asked which areas of knowledge, skills and qualities underpinned effective practice and what the influences on these were. Each of these areas is now summarised.

Table 8.3 – Responsibilities and SMT membership

Responsibility	SMT membership No (%)	Yes (%)
Policy	1 (4.2)	7 (10.9)
Learning	16 (66.7)	17 (26.6)
People	6 (25.0)	27 (42.2)
Resources	0	7 (10.9)
Admin	0	5 (7.8)
Own teaching	1 (4.2)	1 (1.6)
Total	24	64

Table 8.4 – Responsibilities, SMT membership and gender

SMT membership	Women		Men	
Responsibility	No (%)	Yes (%)	No (%)	Yes (%)
Policy	0	3 (9.4)	1 (8.3)	4 (12.5)
Learning	7 (58.3)	10 (31.2)	9 (75.0)	7 (21.9)
People	4 (33.3)	11 (34.4)	2 (16.7)	16 (50.0)
Resources	0	5 (15.6)	0	2 (6.3)
Admin	0	3 (9.4)	0	2 (6.3)
Own teaching	1 (8.3)	0	0	1 (3.1)
Total	12	32	12	32

Knowledge

Again, there was a wide diversity of responses to questions about the knowledge education managers need to carry out their responsibilities. A total of 24 areas were given, the most frequent being 'knowing how the system works' (19), 'about the National Curriculum' (18) and 'about special education' (16). Again, because of the range of answers given it was necessary to group them into categories: educational philosophy, how the school or service works, curriculum, classroom practice, INSET provision and educational evaluation. Table 8.5 shows the distribution of our interviewees' responses into the six categories.

Table 8.5 – Areas of knowledge

Knowledge	Women (%)	Men (%)	All
Educational philosophy	3 (5.3)	10 (23.8)	13
How the school works	17 (29.8)	10 (23.8)	27
Curriculum	5 (8.8)	13 (30.9)	18
Classroom practice	26 (45.6)	7 (16.7)	33
INSET	3 (5.3)	2 (4.8)	5
Evaluation	3 (5.3)	0	3
Total	57	42	99

Men reported more frequently that the knowledge required for their responsibilities concerned educational philosophy and the curriculum, while women more frequently mentioned classroom practice. But their responsibilities were different, so this may account for the differences between the two groups. This question is explored in the next section.

Knowledge and responsibilities

The areas of knowledge were then related to the interviewee's responsibilities. Table 8.6 shows that knowledge from each of the six areas was seen as necessary for most areas of responsibility. The two main areas of responsibility, for managing learning and people, have rather similar profiles, with classroom practice knowledge occurring more often as a requirement for managing learning. Differences between men and women diminish when account is taken of their different pattern of responsibilities: the only remaining difference is in the knowledge required to support responsibilities for learning where the women mention classroom practice more frequently than the men.

Table 8.6 – Knowledge and responsibilities

Knowledge	Responsibilities*			
	Policy (%)	Learning (%)	People (%)	Resources (%)
Ed. philosophy	5 (41.6)	4 (10.5)	3 (8.3)	1 (14.3)
How school works	1 (8.3)	8 (21.1)	8 (22.2)	5 (71.4)
Curriculum	1 (8.3)	9 (23.7)	8 (22.2)	0
Class practice	4 (33.3)	17 (44.7)	11 (30.6)	0
INSET	0	0	4 (11.1)	1 (14.3)
Evaluation	1 (8.3)	0	2 (5.5)	0
Total	12	38	36	7

* The two other areas of responsibility were excluded because of small numbers.

Influences on knowledge

The participants reported influences on their knowledge, skills and qualities. Table 8.7 shows the influences reported on the development of knowledge by gender, and Table 8.8 shows the reported influences on knowledge subdivided by area of responsibility.

Table 8.7 – Influences on knowledge

Influences	Women (%)	Men (%)
Experience in education	29 (26.6)	28 (28.6)
Observing good practice	5 (4.6)	4 (4.1)
LEA courses and practice	19 (17.4)	13 (13.3)
Course elsewhere	11 (10.1)	13 (13.3)
Study/research/reflection	11 (10.1)	5 (5.1)
Experience outside education	3 (2.7)	7 (7.1)
DES documents	3 (2.7)	8 (8.2)
Visiting other schools	2 (1.8)	4 (4.1)
'That sort of person'	1 (0.9)	0
Changes in the law	1 (0.9)	0
MDC course	24 (22.0)	16 (16.3)
Total	109	98

The patterns reported by men and women are quite similar. The main differences between them is that the women report the Centre course as an influence more frequently, and are more influenced by study and research. Table 8.8 shows that the MDC course, and courses elsewhere are more frequently reported as an influence on managing people than on managing learning.

Table 8.8 – The most frequently mentioned influences on knowledge required for managing learning and managing people

	Managing learning %	Managing people %
Experience in education	28.9	2.1
LEA courses and practice	15.6	17.4
Courses elsewhere	8.9	14.5
MDC course	14.4	23.2
Total number of influences reported	90	69

There were slight differences between men and women in their reported influences on knowledge required for managing learning, but not for knowledge required for managing people. For managing learning women reported a greater influence of a Centre course and less from their educational experience generally.

Skills

Thirty one skills were reported. The most frequent individual item was 'communication skills' (17) followed by 'effective implementation skills' (8). Again, because of the diversity of skills reported they had to be grouped into categories for analysis. These were: self-management skills (e.g. time management); working with others (e.g. motivating others); teaching skills (e.g. sensitivity to pupil's needs); and a small number of administrative skills (e.g. computer use). Table 8.9 shows the distribution of skills across the categories. There are very similar patterns for men and women: women mention a slightly higher proportion of 'self-management skills' and slightly fewer 'skills with others'.

Table 8.9 – Skills

Skills	Women (%)	Men (%)	All
Self-management skills	29 (52.7)	25 (44.6)	54
Skills with others	21 (38.2)	26 (46.4)	47
Teaching skills	3 (5.5)	2 (3.4)	5
Admin. skills	2 (3.6)	3 (5.4)	5
Total	55	56	

Skills and responsibilities

Table 8.10 shows interviewees' reports of the skills needed within each area of responsibility.

Table 8.10 – Skills and responsibilities

Skills	Responsibilities*			
	Policy (%)	Learning (%)	People (%)	Resources (%)
Self-management skills	8 (88.9)	23 (48.9)	16 (42.1)	2 (25.0)
Skills with others	1 (11.1)	21 (44.7)	20 (52.6)	3 (37.5)
Teaching skills	0	2 (4.3)	2 (5.3)	0
Admin. skills	0	1 (2.1)	0	3 (37.5)
Total	9	47	38	8

*The two other areas of responsibility were excluded because of small numbers.

Self-management skills were reported more frequently with policy and learning responsibilities, while skills with others was reported for people and resource responsibilities.

Influences on skills

Table 8.11 sets out the interviewees' reports of the influences on their management skills.

Table 8.11 – Influences on skills

Influences	Women (%)	Men (%)
Experience in education	29 (26.4)	32 (26.7)
Observing good practice	12 (10.9)	7 (5.8)
LEA courses and practice	8 (7.3)	11 (9.2)
Course elsewhere	10 (9.1)	12 (10.0)
Study/research/reflection	3 (2.7)	9 (7.5)
Experience outside education	7 (6.4)	7 (5.8)
DES documents	0	1 (0.8)
Visiting other schools	2 (1.8)	1 (0.8)
'That sort of person'	2 (1.8)	6 (5.0)
MDC course	37 (33.6)	34 (28.3)
Total	110	120

Again, the patterns for men and women are similar, with women reporting that the MDC course influenced their skills more often than the men. There were other small differences between men and women: women reported skills being influenced by observing good practice more often than men, while for men there were more frequent reports of influences coming from personal study, and being 'that sort of person'.

Comparing this table with Table 8.7, which shows the influences on knowledge, the Centre courses are mentioned more frequently and other courses less often.

Table 8.12 – The most frequently mentioned influences on skills required for managing learning and managing people

	Managing learning %	Managing people %
Experience in education	30.6	24.4
Observing good managers	9.1	7.7
Courses elsewhere	7.9	11.1
LEA practice and courses	—	7.7
Experience outside education	—	7.7
MDC course	31.8	31.1
Total number of influences reported	88	69

The pattern of influences on men and women in the skills needed for these areas of their work are almost the same.

Qualities

Thirty different qualities were reported. The most frequently mentioned qualities were 'able to get on with others' (13) 'flexible and open minded' (8), and 'being well organised' (8). Because of the diversity of the qualities reported these were divided in two groups: personal qualities (e.g. common sense, clarity of thinking), and inter-personal qualities (e.g. able to get on with others, valuing staff).

Table 8.13 – Qualities

Qualities	Women (%)	Men (%)	All
Personal	29 (63.0)	27 (56.3)	56
Inter-personal	17 (37.0)	21 (43.7)	38
Total	46	48	

Table 8.13 shows that women reported slightly more 'personal' qualities than men.

Table 8.14 – Qualities and responsibilities

Qualities	Responsibilities*			
	Policy (%)	Learning (%)	People (%)	Resources (%)
Personal	6 (85.7)	18 (56.3)	18 (48.6)	9 (90.0)
Inter-personal	1 (14.3)	14 (43.7)	19 (51.4)	1 (10.0)
Total	7	32	37	10

* The two other areas of responsibility were excluded because of small numbers.

Personal qualities were particularly mentioned in relation to managing policy and resources, while both types of qualities were mentioned in relation to managing learning and managing people.

Influences on qualities

Table 8.15 sets out the interviewees' reports of the influences on their management qualities.

Table 8.15 – Influences on qualities

Influences	Women (%)	Men (%)
Experience in education	23 (27.4)	13 (17.3)
Observing good practice	8 (9.5)	7 (9.3)
LEA courses and practice	1 (1.2)	0
Course elsewhere	6 (7.1)	2 (2.7)
Study/research/reflection	2 (2.4)	1 (1.3)
Experience outside education	6 (7.1)	9 (12.0)
DES documents	0	1 (1.3)
Visiting other schools	1 (1.2)	1 (1.3)
'That sort of person'	14 (16.7)	21 (28.0)
MDC course	23 (27.4)	20 (26.6)
Total	84	75

Influences on qualities reported by men and women are similar, with the exception of 'that sort of a person' (given more often by men) and 'experience in education' (given more often by women). The influence of Centre courses is slightly less than that reported on skills.

Table 8.16 – The most frequently mentioned influences on qualities required for managing learning and managing people

	Managing learning %	Managing people %
'That sort of person'	22.2	14.7
Experience in education	18.5	27.9
Experience outside education	13.0	7.4
Observing good managers	—	7.4
Courses elsewhere	—	7.4
MDC course	25.9	32.4
Total number of influences reported	54	68

'Experience in education' and 'that sort of person' are both frequently reported as influences on the development of qualities.

Men and women showed slight differences in their perceived influences on qualities needed to manage learning. Women reported being more influenced by their educational experience and men by being 'that sort of person'. The influences on qualities needed for managing people were also perceived differently: women put more emphasis on both Centre courses and their educational experience while men were more likely to refer to being 'that sort of person'.

Influence of Centre programmes

As part of the interview participants often commented on the ways in the Centre programme enhanced their development as managers. We also have information about the impact of our programmes from the follow-up postal questionnaires. The general themes that emerged will be summarised here.

All interviewees who cited the MDC course as an influence on the development of their knowledge, skills or qualities were asked to describe how they had been influenced. Some could not give a specific response.

Table 8.17 – MDC influences on knowledge, skills and qualities

Aspect of course	Knowledge (%)	Skills (%)	Qualities (%)
Input	15 (39.5)	18 (32.1)	7 (21.9)
Skills practice/role play	8 (21.0)	16 (28.6)	5 (15.6)
Other course members	9 (23.7)	3 (5.4)	5 (15.6)
Time to reflect/self awareness	2 (5.3)	6 (10.7)	6 (18.8)
Ethos/tutors as role models	1 (2.6)	3 (5.4)	3 (9.4)
Work-based project	2 (5.3)	3 (5.4)	2 (6.3)
Increased confidence	1 (2.6)	4 (7.1)	3 (9.4)
Other	0	3 (5.4)	1 (3.1)
Total	38	56	32

Knowledge obtained from the MDC course was reported to have come from inputs, skills practice and other course members; skills from inputs and skills practice; and qualities from inputs, skills practice, other course members and time to reflect.

Increased confidence was also reported in the postal questionnaires. Of the 22 people interviewed, six women and three men mentioned this; they also reported an increased 'sense of direction' as well as management skills such as planning change. These issues will be explored in more detail in future work.

Purposes of the interview study

Five questions were set out at the beginning of this chapter. The research programme reported here has enabled us to begin to answer them.

1. Clear and interesting patterns have emerged concerning the required knowledge, skills and qualities required to be an effective education manager.

2. Interesting patterns have also emerged about the influences on the development of the required knowledge, skills and qualities.
3. The attendance at a Centre course has played a part in participants' development, particularly in the area of management skills. This reflects the intention of our programmes.
4. Men and women differ in their reports of their management responsibilities, and the influences on their development as managers.
5. The interview worked well, and enabled us to collect a rich body of data. Participants enjoyed the interviews and their semi-structured format allowed us to summarise the data obtained.

The future

This interview study is of an untypical group of teachers, chosen because of their willingness to return and sign evaluation questionnaires and to be interviewed. This is quite acceptable for a feasibility study: a larger scale study should include education managers selected from across a wider range, including those who had not taken part in any formal management development programmes. There may also be another, more subtle, bias in this study. Our focus on interpersonal skills and our methods of working are clearly set out in our literature. This may result in us recruiting an atypical group of participants — less committed to a 'managerial' model, perhaps?

Knowledge, skills and qualities, as defined by our interviewees, sometimes overlapped. In this chapter their own definitions were used. We need to explore teachers' perceptions of these, and of their management role in more detail.

This chapter gives some indications of the developmental process teachers move through in their professional lives. In order to understand how they develop as managers we need to understand their perceptions of 'chains of development'. Which experiences lead to which outcomes and is this dependent on the teachers own current role or experience? We are particularly interested in the most effective way of supporting management development through teachers' careers. At what stage is a school-based development contract, or mentoring, or a management course for example, the most appropriate?

We are also interested in exploring the particular role that might be played by a Management Centre such as ours. While recognising the importance of school-based INSET in many areas of teachers' professional development, it seems likely that cluster, LEA or HE-based programmes will continue to offer opportunities for management development which cannot be met by the individual school.

Acknowledgements

We would like to thank the Baring Foundation for their generous support without which this study would not have been possible. We would also like to thank the teachers who so willingly gave time to talk about their professional development.

References

Alexander, R. (1991) *Primary Education in Leeds: Briefing and Summary* Leeds: University of Leeds School of Education.
Department of Education and Science (1991) *Developing School Management: the way forward* London: HMSO.
Department of Education and Science (1992) *Statistics of Education: Schools* London: DES.
Earley, P. (1991) 'Defining and assessing school management competences' *Management in Education* **5**,(4), 31–34.
Kolb, D.A. (1984) *Experiential Learning: Experience as a Source of Learning and Development* Englewood Cliffs, NJ: Prentice Hall.
Ouston, J. (1993) 'Management competences, school effectiveness and education management' *Educational Management and Administration* (accepted for publication).
School Management South (1992) *School Management Competences Project* Crawley: SMS.

9 Management development for women in a non-educational setting — the BBC experience

Anne Segall

Introduction

In this chapter I look at the history of women's development in the BBC and at why personal and corporate development initiatives for women are important both for individuals and for the organisation as a whole.

I am aware that I write against a background of contracting employment opportunities and increased competition between organisations in all sectors of industry. This is a scenario as real for the BBC as it is for any other public or indeed, private organisation and it is one that has encouraged many companies to take a short-term view, which emphasises the need to increase the 'bottom-line' and which ignores, or at best marginalises, employees' long-term development goals.

I argue that for the BBC, for educational establishments and for organisations generally this is a blinkered approach. If we do not encourage women, and indeed all employees, to develop their skills in the workplace then companies in the future will be devoid of creative managers who can manage the complex problems and issues that organisations and society face as we approach the 21st century.

Personal development and the development of women in particular, must, therefore, remain a key area of activity for the BBC and what is true for the BBC should also be true for women in other areas of working life, and in education in particular. It is to be hoped, therefore, that future initiatives which are being considered for women in the BBC will also be taken up elsewhere and that, in turn, the BBC can learn from management initiatives being taken in other areas of public life.

Background

Since World War II Britain has undergone the most dramatic change in its cultural and ethnic make-up. It has changed from a white Anglo-Saxon, male dominated, culture to a multi-racial society where the subject of equality of opportunity for women, and for minority groups, is firmly on the agenda. These post-war changes have been driven by the demand for a revision of the traditional roles performed by men and women, both in the workplace and in society in general.

Slowly at first and then gathering more speed with the establishment of the women's movement, women began to broaden their horizons and demand fulfilling careers away from their accepted domestic role as wives and mothers or as participants in the 'caring or support professions' such as nurses, social workers, secretaries etc.

Organisations began to be affected as these developments gathered momentum and legislation was introduced to promote the equal employment of racial minorities and of women. What was true for other organisations was also true for the BBC.

Although the BBC had always considered itself an equal opportunities employer, by the early 1980s it was evident that it found itself lagging behind in the employment and promotion of both women and minority groups in relation to the size of these populations in the country as a whole. With the increasing number of younger women and those from ethnic minority groups to consider and the social responsibility towards the disabled the time was right for the BBC to initiate action in the field of equal opportunities.

One of the first outcomes of this concern was the commissioning of a report for the Board of Governors on women and top jobs in the BBC. The report, by Monica Sims, focused on the fact that even though women were entering the BBC's training schemes in larger numbers than ever before, in the highest grades the proportion of men and women had remained much the same as it had been some ten years before. This was a situation which could not be allowed to continue and there were three main reasons for this:

1. At the most 'basic' level equal opportunities policy advocates that women need to be employed on an equal footing with

men and given the same opportunities to progress their careers. In the early 1980s this was not necessarily the case.

2. By not promoting women their potential contribution was being lost, at a time of increased competition in the industry, when creative solutions to complex issues were needed more and more.
3. Without women in top jobs there were no 'role models' for women further down the Corporation and so they were unable to benefit from the experience of those who had 'gone before'.

   Without female 'role models' it was thought that the cycle of inequality would be perpetuated.

This is not to say that role models are the *only* factor in promoting women's development. Others such as:

- the working environment;
- commitment from top managers to develop women;
- child care and other provisions, e.g. flexible working, job sharing;
- increased training opportunities;

are equally important. But having role models to learn from in terms of negative and positive experiences, has been shown to be a key factor in promoting the progress of women in the workplace.

The current situation

Women now make up approximately 43 per cent of the BBC's staff which is equivalent to the proportion of women in the labour market as a whole. Women, however, predominate in lower paid jobs although their representation in management and production *has* steadily improved during the 1980s. There are now 26 per cent of women in the top management grades as opposed to 16 per cent in 1987 and 7 per cent in 1982.

The BBC has also stated that its aim is to:

> reflect in its workforce, the nation it serves by the year 2000. This acknowledges that it is only by making use of all available talent that the best programmes will be made to meet the needs of all sections of the community.

Indeed, to substantiate this commitment in 1990 the BBC set itself targets for the employment of women in management positions for the year 1996. These targets are 30 per cent for the most senior posts and 40 per cent for the next two grades. In 1996 it is intended to review the situation and, in the light of the progress made, set further targets for the year 2000.

The introduction of targets gives the BBC an aim and a goal in terms of equality of opportunity. But, without practical initiatives to back these targets and real commitment to achieve them they become little more than a paper exercise.

It is, therefore, important to look behind the targets and see what is really being done for women's development into management positions in the BBC.

Towards a more equitable future — BBC initiatives promoting management development for women

The BBC's Staff Development Department oversees two key development programmes whose aim is to positively encourage women to progress their careers within the organisation. These are:

1. The Women's Development Programme aimed at women in junior and non-management grades.
2. Women in Management for women in management grades from all areas of the BBC. This course is aimed at a wide spectrum of women from those who have only just entered a 'managing role' to those who have progressed to middle and senior management positions.

The next section looks at how these programmes have been set-up and at the learning and development that has resulted from them.

Personal development initiatives

The Women's Development Programme

The BBC had always run 'traditional' management courses which were skill and theory based and 'taught' the background needed for managers to manage in, what was, a hierachical, bureaucratic organisation. Until the late 1980s however, little was done in the field of personal development and there were no formal initiatives to enable groups of junior staff to look at their future progress and aspirations.

Progress for women into management, therefore, happened very much on an ad hoc basis. Individual women would succeed because of their own skill at promoting themselves and because of the 'informal' (and sometimes formal) support they gained from senior managers, personnel officers and, in some cases, from individual mentors.

The BBC's recruitment and selection procedures were (and are) based on open competition. All jobs and short-term secondments (or attachments) are advertised each week in the staff newspaper and all staff are able to apply for jobs, for which they are suitably qualified, having completed one year's employment.

This system has had the benefit of opening up advancement to all staff but where women lacked (and still lack) the skills necessary to compete on an equal footing with men they can be placed at a disadvantage. As the 1980s saw the opening up of the debate on equal opportunities, and the appointment of the first Equal Opportunities Officer for the Corporation, it became clear that something had to be done to help women gain the skills they needed to successfully compete for management positions.

It also became evident that programmes were required not just for those in senior positions but also for those lower down the Corporation structure. Helping these women would encourage them to develop the skills they would need to enter management positions and also provide them with advice and guidance on how to effectively manage their careers. This was something that had never been undertaken before in any sort of systematic way.

So, in 1988 the BBC commissioned Liz Willis and Jenny Daisley of Springboard Consultancy to begin working with a cross-section of BBC women on the introduction of a development programme aimed at women in non-managerial grades. The programme was titled The Women's Development Programme and the first event was run early in 1989.

As this was a pioneering initiative the format and content was of the utmost importance. A vast amount of research was, therefore, undertaken to ensure that the formula was one that would appeal to women and be relevent for their progress both into management grades and for their own personal development, both inside and outside the work environment.

The agreed format was for three one day workshops run 4–6 weeks apart. These are now run on average four times a year with up to 70 women attending each programme. The workshops are supported by an open learning journal entitled *Signpost* which the women complete between the workshops.

There was, from the start, a realisation that simply attending a course and coming away with a folder and textbook that could be placed on a shelf and never read again, was not going to be sufficient to promote *real* learning and development. The three workshop events backed by the journal were seen as a way of overcoming this, all too familiar, training dilemma. The core principle has been to give women more than just a course — instead it is hoped they go away with a sense of personal development that stays with them for all time and which will lead them to progress their careers within the BBC.

Many factors contribute to the formula outlined above. Perhaps, most importantly are the women themselves. The 70 delegates come from all areas of the BBC from jobs such as: secretaries, administrative clerks, technical assistants and researchers. The support and encouragement they give each other is one of the key features of the programme. During the workshops delegates are split into groups of 10 to complete exercises and these groups often meet up during the three months to complete portions of the open learning materials.

Workshop 1

This is an introductory day. The women meet each other and have a chance to look at their aims for the three months. The *Signpost* Journal is given out and information exchanged on how best to complete it.

While there is a set timetable for the day the women are encouraged to participate at all times and present the work they do in syndicates to the whole group. This is very much a participatory programme and not a 'chalk and talk' lecture. For many women it will be the first time they have ever spoken in public and the support and motivation from their colleagues to 'have a go' is one of the highlights of the programme. The emphasis then is very much on 'empowerment' and boosting confidence. Help, support and advice is available and the programme is fundamentally saying:

> the future is in your hands here are the tools to make the most of it, now it's up to you.

Workshop 2

The second workshop is run some six weeks after the first. During that time women have completed several chapters in the journal looking at their skills, interests, balance of work and home life and setting some future goals. The emphasis is on taking small steps one at a time and celebrating achievements. This, in particular, is something that woman, in general, do not do enough of.

There is also encouragement for trying something new, for example, buying a different newspaper from the one individual delegates normally read or taking up that new hobby they have been thinking about for years. Again, the support of other women is a key factor here in terms of maintaining impetus and motivation.

At the start of workshop two groups of women speak about the successes they have had since they last met and what they are hoping to achieve in the future. The programme then goes on to look at the blockages to women's advancement and how to overcome them. It is here that much time is spent on assertiveness, influencing and negotiating. Role plays are used to help women practice overcoming difficult situations and feedback is given on their style during afternoon coaching sessions.

Assertiveness was made such a strong feature of the programme because most BBC women when questioned said 'it wasn't that opportunities weren't there for them it was that they didn't know how to go after them or make an impact when they were being overlooked'.

Other women reported that they didn't know that opportunities existed and this, it appears, is often one of the problems of corporate communication in an organisation as large as the BBC. Information on career opportunities and further training and study is, therefore, made available on the programme and contact names and numbers given.

Workshop 3

The final workshop is devoted to the subject of 'how to sell yourself'. Now that delegates have all the information they need and have thought about what they want to do, time can be spent on the best way to promote themselves. At the end of the programme women set action plans and keep their journals to refer to and work with whenever they might need them. Many women decide to link up afterwards and successful women's networks have been set up across the country.

A career session is also included in this workshop focusing on the background and techniques needed to get a new job. Additionally, each workshop features at least one half hour talk by a senior BBC women on how they have managed their career.

This session called 'Footsteps in the Snow' is not simply 'this is how I succeeded, now you do the same'. Instead each women is asked to discuss the highlights and lowlights of their career and how they have dealt with them. This use of 'role modelling' has helped many junior women with their own decision-making process. Past delegates also act as helpers and can be phoned during or after the programme for guidance and advice.

The programme has been dubbed 'not so much a training course' more a way of life' and certainly it is seen as a start on the road to future development rather than a complete training programme which ends on the last workshop.

The inclusion of the journal has also been a key feature. Women have the chance to work on it in their own time and to use it to deal with work based issues and problems. In many cases this has resulted in women initiating discussions with senior colleagues and managers which they would not have otherwise had.

The promotion of discussion and networking was an important requirement at the initial design stage as was the need to ensure that the programme was relevant to all the women that attended. It was noted from the outset that adults have different learning styles and so Kolb's work on learning styles as adapted by Honey and Mumford, was given consideration at this stage. The programme includes role plays, presentations and discussions that appeal to activists, work-based information and problem solving for pragmatists and the journal and articles for reflectors and theorists.

To date, more than 1,000 women have attended the programme and facilitation of the workshops is now undertaken by a group of women who attended the first programme and expressed an interest in being trained as facilitators. This has helped with their own personal development and gives the BBC a group of trained women who are experienced in presentation and have substantial knowledge and experience to guide more junior women to future success.

A recent evaluation of the programme produced the following data:

- 88 per cent of the women questioned said the programme had made a difference to their lives. It had encouraged them to feel positive and to undertake new activities that they wouldn't have done before.
- 70 per cent of women said they had gone into new jobs or training or changed direction as a result of the programme. Information given on the programme about career breaks, job sharing and secondments had also been acted on.

In summary the programme has helped women become more focused and has encouraged them to cultivate a positive attitude in their work and personal lives. Certainly, many managers questioned said they had noticed a difference in the way those who had attended the programme approached their work.

This is a particularly important point. Obviously, to run a programme of this nature within an organisation it is important that both the individual and the organisation benefit in terms of meeting future work based objectives.

Looking at previous feedback this has been achieved, and it is, therefore, going to be crucial to ensure that the programme stays relevant both for women and for the BBC as a whole.

With the increased emphasis on rationalisation and recent redundancies and cutbacks it can be easy for managers to say: 'I need my staff at work not out on training courses. I don't want them to think about moving on and developing, I need them here to help fulfil the business plan'.

An important task for the next months and years will be to help managers see the benefits of developing staff in terms of their increased motivation and initiative in the workplace and, as a consequence, help them look at long term development as a necessity, not just for the individual concerned, but for the BBC as a whole. In this way, the Women's Development Programme in particular, will be able to continue playing a key role in introducing and preparing junior women for future management positions.

Women in Management

The Women's Development Programme is a positive initiative to help women develop their work and personal life. The aim of Women in Management is similar but the debate is taken on a stage.

This programme runs as a three day block for up to 20 delegates and is held four times a year. The numbers are kept down to encourage a lively and informative debate.

The women who attend have in some instances attended the Women's Development Programme but more often than not have either been on a management skills based programme or have received only technical training in their particular area of expertise.

The delegates then, come from different backgrounds with disparate experiences of training but with one aim in mind.

> What does it mean to be a women manager in the BBC, how does this balance with my domestic life and do I want to progress further?

The programme is structured (albeit flexibly!) around these major concerns.

As with the Women's Development Programme workshops the course is participative and begins on day one looking at the delegates career to date.

Where have I been and who and what has helped me? is a key question of the day. Use is also made of Schultz's FIRO-B questionnaire to help delegates raise their awareness of their own individual style at work.

Day 2 takes the delegates on a stage further to look at themselves as managers. The day's theme is how do I manage in the workplace and is this a fulfilling experience?

Many women feel that the only way to progress their careers is to act 'like men'. This, for them, means using a domineering, telling approach based on the acquisition of power. Not only do the majority of women who attend not feel comfortable using this style but they believe it is 'manipulative' and often counter-productive. The dilemma they are left with is if they don't adopt such a style can they progress. Here the programme is able to help them by developing two separate, yet inter-related themes:

1. How to cultivate an effective style that is right for the individual and that is going to be effective in a work situation.
2. The whole issue of using personal power is discussed and exercises are undertaken to help women feel more comfortable both with the term and its use in the workplace.

Day 3 concentrates on drawing on the experience and knowledge gained on the programme and setting goals for the future. Particular attention is given to looking at the balance between women's home and working lives and what that means for their careers. The women are encouraged to share their experiences and learn from one another.

Feedback from the programme has constantly shown that women find the event a postive one. Many say it has come at a time of their life when they needed to make choices about where they are going and what they want to do, and that the programme has helped them face some difficult decisions. The women are encouraged to go back and talk to their own managers about their experiences and the fulfilment of their work based development goals. Many managers report that women come back with renewed motivation and a better sense of their individual management style and how to use it.

Again, the programme encourages networking as a central theme and many women report that they have achieved further career progress as a result of meeting women on the programme.

Individual coaching and counselling is also offered as follow up to the women if they require it. Approximately 50 per cent take up this offer.

The programme is structured as one block of three days because it has been found that this helps the delegates to focus. Most have extremely demanding jobs and it is doubtful whether they would be able to attend a course split over a number of weeks.

So, while they differ in structure and content both programmes are major initiatives to encourage women's development in the BBC. There is, however, another dimension to development which cannot be overlooked and that is the part that the organisation plays in assisting women to obtain management positions. Diagramatically it can be represented as in Figure 9.1.

The ideal development line is achieved when the individual is being developed and the organisational systems are in place to ensure that development takes place in a systematic way with benefit to the organisation as well as to the individual.

Without these systems in place, training courses, open learning packages and development programmes cannot show positive results. Individuals will have had their expectations raised but if they are returned to an imperfect system then it is doubtful whether they will make any progress and will almost certainly become disillusioned and demotivated.

This scenario also sees the organisation making a net loss. Money is lost on development programmes because the plans the delegates make (which will benefit both the individuals concerned and the organisation) cannot be put into place.

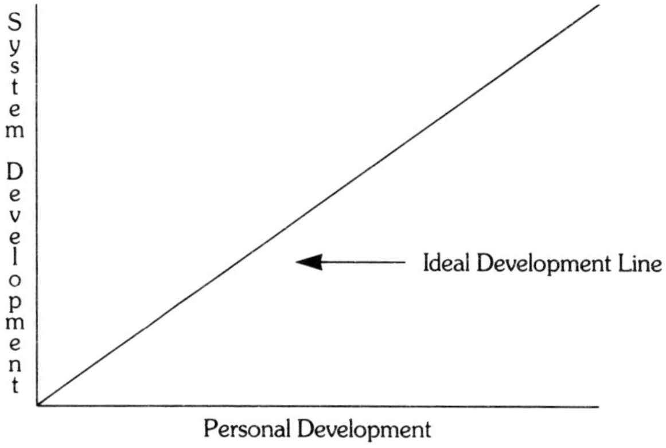

Figure 9.1

It is important, therefore, to look at what the BBC has done in terms of establishing systems that will help women develop within the Corporation.

Systems development

The BBC agreed an equal opportunities policy statement in 1983 and reviewed and updated it in 1991. It is this policy which forms the basis of equal opportunities action and initiatives within the Corporation. This policy and the BBC's commitment to equal opportunities is constantly reaffirmed and publicised both internally and externally. Thus, giving women the impetus to apply for development programmes.

A fair and equitable recruitment policy has been put in place to back-up this policy and all managers who interview staff are provided with Fair Selection Training to ensure fair treatment.

It could be argued that simply providing systems is in itself not enough, as all systems are only as good as those that administer them. The BBC therefore, systematically monitors both its workforce and its recruitment and selection procedures in order to identify where 'blockages' occur for women and areas where they are under represented. For example, in 1986 an 'operational awareness' course was set up, designed to give women working in administrative and secretarial jobs the opportunity of experiencing the work of camera operators, vision mixers and sound operators. Women had been under-represented in technical categories until this point and the course is seen as a way of positively preparing them for future opportunities in these areas.

Perhaps, though, the greatest block of all on women progressing into management grades is the need to balance home and work life. Often the time when women are ready to move into management postions is also the time they are thinking of starting a family. It is certainly true that in the past in large and small organisations alike, this has been a major obstacle in the path of women's development. Last year the Institute of Management produced a study on Women in Management and found that nearly half of the women they questioned, who had had children, said their careers had been adversely affected.

Giving up work to have children, for however short a period is a real dilemma for women that has not yet been properly addressed by organisations in this country. This problem is often compounded by the disproportionate share of domestic responsibilities that women still undertake. It is a sad conclusion that until this situation is fully addressed by organisations, by governments and by society in general, many women will never have the opportunity to reach their true potential.

For the BBC's part, since the mid 1980s it has been embarking on a series of initiatives to help alleviate this situation for its staff. These include:

- nursery provision at six BBC locations;
- holiday play schemes, run during school holidays for children from five to 12 years old;
- job sharing guidelines (produced in 1986) and a policy (1989); there are now job sharers in all areas of the BBC;
- a career-break scheme introduced in 1987 and parent support groups on most BBC sites.

These initiatives obviously go some way to helping women combine work and domestic routines. Yet, for many they do not go far enough and in the future it is going to be necessary for the BBC to encourage further flexible working arrangements to enable all employees to combine work and home responsibilities.

There is, however, no doubting the BBC's aim and commitment to changing the relative proportions of men and women at the top levels of the Corporation and to introduce more women into management. To do this effectively it is going to have to regularly review progress and use active human resource planning to help identify ways forward. In addition, it must listen to what women themselves say on development programmes, and in any surveys carried out, so that future initiatives can be focused and relevant. This raises some further, interesting questions about the future role and progression of women in the BBC.

What is the future for women's development in the BBC?

It would appear at first sight that the future for women in the BBC is assured. There are systems in place to assist their career development and courses to help boost their confidence and help them plan for the future. Yet, many women, when questioned, are still unhappy with the status quo. The main problem as outlined earlier is one of the style they perceive they need to acquire in order to progress.

This can best be described as a traditional male style based on controlling, power, telling and assuming leadership and authority. Historically this model has been paramount in organisations and indeed, in western society in general. It is a style of management which is linked to a hierarchical model of organisational structure, familiar in business as the 'traditional' way of structuring work.

One strategy for managing this tension for women is to copy male behaviour, attitudes and values. It has been shown that behaving closely similar to men will earn them acceptance and they may well be highly successful in terms of promotions. Indeed, this policy is favoured in much of the management literature. Many of the suggestions offered in the literature for how to increase the number and prospects for women in management jobs concentrate on how to socialise women to behave like men. Indeed, single sex training is often seen as a way of educating women to learn to play the male 'game' at work. Women are encouraged to 'learn the rules' to 'use power' to be 'more assertive'.

Yet, this style does not appear a relevant one for men or women in the current environment. The changes that are being brought about in BBC culture and structure, in particular, mean that for both men and women a new style of management is emerging. This change (towards a less hierarchical, centralised organisation) is being mirrored in many companies across the UK and the change is critical if they are to compete and succeed in the present climate.

The result of this is to make the 1990s a decade in which business has begun to value different styles. Many companies, and I would include the BBC here, have come to believe that the best way to motivate people comes from a consultative, approachable style of management based on genuine two-way communication. Perhaps the shock of so many executives retiring early or dying on the job has helped to drive home the message that people and their relationships are critical factors in achieving organisational goals. Budget and control are important issues but so too is the person who ties them together.

Coupled with this approach, a new way of working is emerging which is also helping to break down the more traditional system of managing. More and more often the numbers of employees at the 'core' of businesses are being reduced, and services are being brought in from individuals who have an association with a company but who are not tied into its structure in the longer term. Certainly this is a scenario often quoted in the current literature and which can be seen emerging in the BBC.

For this situation a different style of management is needed. The use of co-ordinating, consulting and mediating management skills will be in greater demand than ever. These are skills which are traditionally associated with women managers and indeed the vast majority of current management skills programmes are intent on training managers to learn and promote new ways of working in accordance with these changes.

The future may well see a situation where men and women are no longer penalised by the old stereotypes of male and female behaviour and where they can develop skills in keeping with their management role in organisations.

How managers perform in their roles will then become a question which is determined by a number of crucial variables apart from the 'soft' and 'hard' styles traditionally associated with gender. These variables include:

- the ability managers have to take risks, to be entreprenurial, and progress business;
- the type of environment in which the organisation operates;
- the culture of the organisation;
- the time pressures in the job; and
- the management style of senior management.

Perhaps though, above all, the closest factor to determining performance is the personality of the individual manager.

Measuring individuals' natural work preferences provides an extremely useful way of identifying how they are likely to perform in their jobs. Help and training can then be given to enable them to develop skills and competencies that they are missing or behaviours which they find difficult to express.

Indeed, the BBC is shortly to set up its first Assessment Development Centre to do just this.

Using this approach takes us out of the realms of how men and women are stereotyped as working and what that perception means in practice, into the arena of how we would like to work.

Progress perhaps is slow (but sure) in terms of changing the way managers manage, but this progress does mean that female managers can begin to think differently about what is expected from them at work and how they will have to operate to succeed.

It is to be hoped that through understanding and a will to change it will be possible to gain a better balance of male/female values, attitudes and behaviours not only from individual managers within the BBC, but more widely in other organisations, communities and in society as a whole.

The development of all human resources depends on a greater awareness of what possibilities, qualities, aptitudes and abilities really exist within our organisations and this, in turn, leads to the following question:

> How do we harness the resources present in all managers — female and male — and help them work effectively, so they can fulfill their own personal development plans and contribute to organisational success?

The answer may vary from organisation to organisation depending on their stage of development and the individuals who run them. What is certain is that this is a question that has to be addressed if there is to be progress towards even greater equality of opportunity and business success for individual companies.

The whole field of future work-based relationships and self-development and learning will depend on the need for an accurate assessment of where managers and potential managers are, the nature of their individual goals and of their organisation's objectives. As women and men involved in education, training and development, it is important to be a part of this assessment, not only to increase our own understanding but also to help us help individuals with their development. Perhaps even more fundamentally we must listen to what individuals say to us and act on their suggestions and ideas. We also need to help build relationships to engender trust and confidence, and the kind of organisations where people are not afraid to speak out, or tell it as it really is. In short there is a vital role to be played in helping men and women achieve organisational change. A change based on a new style of managing that can deal with power and control in a balanced way; that is comfortable with the full range of human emotions; that can seek support and give it to others; that can be independent without being isolated and can acknowledge attraction and choose whether to act on it or not. Such a manager is better equipped to face the challenges of these complex economic times.

Such a job spec, based on equality of opportunity and with the necessary supporting structures in place, would attract more women into management than ever before. This is part of the BBC's aim. A recent report stated that 'The BBC wishes to optimise staff development and effectiveness across the Corporation'.

The way forward must be to make the best of all the BBC's staff and from this course of action encourage women to pursue management careers. Failure to promote women will lead to loss of potential at a time when the BBC and indeed other companies across the UK, can ill afford to do so. It would also deprive future generations of the role models they need to help them succeed in organisations such as the BBC.

Concluding remarks

The foregoing has important implications for both the BBC's Women's Development and Women in Management Programmes.

Both programmes emphasise the need for women to 'manage in their own right' and they are based firmly on the need for female managers and potential managers to find:

1. an acceptable balance between home and paid work; and
2. the style of management that best suits them and their work commitments.

In this way the programmes avoid the criticism often levelled at single sex training, that they simply tell women how to play a game of domination at work.

Any future redesign would, therefore, have to continue to look at the whole person and how women can operate most effectively both in the work environment and in life in general.

Other topics for redesign will also include looking at how to manage yourself effectively in a continually changing, stressful environment. More work on balancing home and paid work and perhaps most importantly current thinking on negotiating, influencing and using personal power effectively. These topics together with those skills covered on the 'traditional' management skills programmes, will ensure women in the BBC are equiped to face the changing demands and needs of the organisation while taking heed of their own personal development goals.

Perhaps for some time to come women will want to work on their own to tackle these issues, depending on their level of development and confidence. I would also like to think that it is possible to go further than this. If there are issues that women still need to tackle, whatever these may be, from managing change in the workplace to how home life affects their job performance, then space should be given to them to underake these explorations on development courses. If women are not fulfilled in terms of this personal development how can they be expected to play a full role in the workplace?

What is not on the agenda at present is a mixed programme where men and women could look at their relationships at work and at how they can work more effectively together. Perhaps, when women are ready and conditions are right, there will be a move away from single sex training towards a learning or training event of this nature. Here men and women could share their concerns about current issues and learn different styles of behaviour from each other which could help them manage more efficiently in the workplace. It would also give them the opportunity to share their experience of work and to encourage each other in their development goals.

It may be that initially this would be a course that would run alongside single sex training, to complement it until such time as it is perceived that single sex training is no longer relevant or necessary. It would also be good to think that when this time comes it will be judged to be the right time by both organisations and perhaps more importantly, by the women who have benefited from single sex training.

This scenario takes us full circle, because no further training or learning opportunities are going to be given in the workplace in any organisations in the present climate, unless they can be justified. As has been stated, many businesses are now looking to the short-term bottom line and personal development goals and the need for holistic development do not necessarily fit comfortably with this bottom line approach.

It must, therefore, be argued strongly that all members of a company's workforce must be developed in the longer-term if companies are to be successful. To achieve this a compromise may well have to be reached between the short-term bottom line and longer term development needs. But this cannot and should not be allowed to be at the expense of longer term individual development needs.

The challenge ahead should not be underestimated. There are still many difficulties which individual women will face entering traditional male preserves and the higher echelons of management both in the BBC, in education and in other large organisations, be they in the public or private sector. It is, therefore, not going to be enough merely to attract more women into management jobs through training programmes. What will be equally important is to recognise and understand their difficulties and give them the support they need to become effective and successful. If this support is taken further and can be offered to all staff then organisations really will have a chance of surviving the current climate of uncertainty and emerge stronger and more productive than they ever have been.

It is, therefore, to be hoped that the cost of ignoring the future development of managers (and of female managers, in particular) is one that the BBC, and indeed all organisations in the UK, decide is too great to bear.

Note

The views expressed in this chapter are my own and do not constitute BBC policy.

Index